Tell me the story of Jesus, Write on my heart every word;
Tell me the story most precious, Sweetest that ever was heard.
Tell how the angels in chorus, Sang as they welcomed His birth,
Glory to God in the highest! Peace and good tidings to earth.

Fasting alone in the desert, Tell of the days that are past,
How for our sins He was tempted, Yet was triumphant at last.
Tell of the years of His labor, Tell of the sorrow He bore,
He was despised and afflicted, Homeless, rejected and poor.

Tell of the cross where they nailed Him, Writhing in anguish and pain;
Tell of the grave where they laid Him, Tell how He liveth again.
Love in that story so tender, Clearer than ever I see:
Stay, let me weep while you whisper, Love paid the ransom for me.

—Fanny J. Crosby*

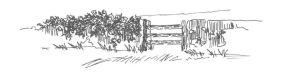

20th Anniversary Edition

# Joni Eareckson Tada

## 2004 Planner

World Wide Publications
Charlotte, North Carolina 28266

**2004 Joni Planner**
**Wire-O Paperback Edition**

© 2003 Joni Eareckson Tada

Cover illustration by Joni Eareckson Tada

In compliance with copyright restrictions, no portion of these materials may be reproduced in any form without written permission of the publisher: World Wide Publications, P.O. Box 669007, Charlotte, North Carolina 28266-9007.

World Wide Publications is the publishing ministry of the Billy Graham Evangelistic Association.

Unless otherwise noted, Scripture quotations are taken from the *Holy Bible, New International Version.* © 1973, 1978, 1984 International Bible Society. Used by permission of Zondervan Bible Publishers.

ISBN: 0-89066-340-8

Printed in Canada.

# Joni Eareckson Tada

If you want to keep up with Joni these days, you'll have to run fast—her wheelchair's in high gear as she travels the world, sharing the Good News of Jesus Christ with thousands of families affected by disability. She slows down when she gets home, however. And on most weekends, you can still catch Joni in the quiet solitude of her art studio as she sits at her easel, painting and drawing while holding the brushes between her teeth.

"I'm so excited about my *2004 Planner*," Joni says. "This year marks the 20th anniversary of this special series. For the past two decades, it's been the joy of my heart to render paintings and write devotionals for my Planners. And my heart still overflows whenever I receive warm and encouraging letters from people who enjoy them—I heard from a woman who has been using my Planners since 1984; she's placed them on her shelf as a kind of family encyclopedia!"

For the *2004 Planner*, Joni has selected Bible verses and quotes which underscore the "old, old story of Jesus and his love." In our hurried, fast-paced world, we can find quiet peace and calm serenity as we focus on the basics—the story of Jesus and his awe-inspiring love. Joni says, "The older I get in the Lord, the less complicated, the less cluttered my life of faith seems to be. My ministry may have me running fast, but my walk with Jesus continues in slow, sure, steady steps. It's so *good* to keep in measured step with the Spirit."

You will enjoy the daily reminders of the old gospel story which Joni has penned into this year's Planner. She has authored thirty books including the latest, her memoir, *The God I Love,* published by Zondervan. She also serves as the president of Joni and Friends, an international Christian organization which accelerates Christian ministry into the disability community. For more information on Joni's Christmas cards, write to Grason at P.O. Box 669007, Charlotte, NC 28266-9007 or e-mail grasoncs@bgea.org. For more information on Joni's disability outreach, contact Joni and Friends, P.O. Box 3333, Agoura Hills, CA 91376 or visit their Web site at www.joniandfriends.org.

# Uncle Eddie's Skis

Whenever I see the snow swirl in January, I always remember a long-ago afternoon when I had just come home from the hospital. I was sitting in my wheelchair by the window, watching the big flakes and feeling sorry for myself. I was stuck inside and keenly aware that I was unable to enjoy all the activities I used to. I was convinced I could no longer sleigh ride, make snowmen, skate, or throw snowballs.

Suddenly, my Uncle Eddie burst into the house with his son, Eddie, Jr., carrying a big package. "Look!" he beamed, "I've made you a pair of skis!" My uncle—who at that time worked as an engineer for Westinghouse—had fashioned a pair of wide, flat metal skis with small runners to hold the wheels of my wheelchair. "Let's try them out!" he said.

The next thing I knew, I was bundled up and sitting at the top of the snow-covered hill outside my home with my uncle and cousin securing my wheels to the skis. With a whoop and a holler, we pushed off—me, sailing down the hill, laughing and giggling, and Uncle Eddie alongside, running to keep up.

That cold January day was a turning point for me emotionally. Yes, the metal skis did a lot to lift my spirits. But it was my uncle's thoughtfulness which made the difference. A person who has the gift of encouragement can stand back, assess a situation, then put on the thinking cap to come up with a creative suggestion, if not solution. An *encouraging* solution! It's just what I needed that cold, snowy January afternoon.

Although I've forgotten so much of the sadness during those early days of my paralysis, there's one thing I will always remember: my dear Uncle Eddie and the warm gift of his encouragement.

# January Planner
### Goals

National Eye Care Month
National Hot Tea Month

### Prayer Requests

### Bible Reading & Study

### People to See & Calls to Make

### Birthdays & Special Days

# January *2004*

| Sunday | Monday | Tuesday | Wednesday |
|--------|--------|---------|-----------|
|        |        |         |           |
| 4 | 5 | 6 | 7 |
| 11 | 12 | 13 | 14 |
| 18 | 19<br>Martin Luther King Jr.'s<br>Birthday Observed | 20 | 21 |
| 25 | 26 | 27 | 28 |

| Thursday | Friday | Saturday |
|---|---|---|
| 1<br>New Year's Day | 2 | 3 |
| 8 | 9 | 10 |
| 15 | 16 | 17 |
| 22 | 23 | 24 |
| 29 | 30 | 31 |

DECEMBER 2003

| S | M | T | W | T | F | S |
|---|---|---|---|---|---|---|
|  |  | 1 | 2 | 3 | 4 | 5 | 6 |
| 7 | 8 | 9 | 10 | 11 | 12 | 13 |
| 14 | 15 | 16 | 17 | 18 | 19 | 20 |
| 21 | 22 | 23 | 24 | 25 | 26 | 27 |
| 28 | 29 | 30 | 31 |  |  |  |

FEBRUARY

| S | M | T | W | T | F | S |
|---|---|---|---|---|---|---|
| 1 | 2 | 3 | 4 | 5 | 6 | 7 |
| 8 | 9 | 10 | 11 | 12 | 13 | 14 |
| 15 | 16 | 17 | 18 | 19 | 20 | 21 |
| 22 | 23 | 24 | 25 | 26 | 27 | 28 |
| 29 |  |  |  |  |  |  |

# January

**Prayer Requests**

The LORD is my strength and my song;
he has become my salvation. He is my God,
and I will praise him, my father's God,
and I will exalt him.
*Exodus 15:2*

---

**28** SUNDAY · *DECEMBER*

---

**29** MONDAY

---

**30** TUESDAY

## 31 WEDNESDAY
**New Year's Eve**

### JANUARY
| S | M | T | W | T | F | S |
|---|---|---|---|---|---|---|
|   |   |   |   | 1 | 2 | 3 |
| 4 | 5 | 6 | 7 | 8 | 9 | 10 |
| 11 | 12 | 13 | 14 | 15 | 16 | 17 |
| 18 | 19 | 20 | 21 | 22 | 23 | 24 |
| 25 | 26 | 27 | 28 | 29 | 30 | 31 |

### FEBRUARY
| S | M | T | W | T | F | S |
|---|---|---|---|---|---|---|
| 1 | 2 | 3 | 4 | 5 | 6 | 7 |
| 8 | 9 | 10 | 11 | 12 | 13 | 14 |
| 15 | 16 | 17 | 18 | 19 | 20 | 21 |
| 22 | 23 | 24 | 25 | 26 | 27 | 28 |
| 29 |   |   |   |   |   |   |

## 1 THURSDAY · JANUARY
**New Year's Day**

*Choose an annual verse for 2004 . . .*

## 2 FRIDAY

*Memorize it . . .*

## 3 SATURDAY

*Make it your resolution!*

# January

**Prayer Requests**

*Hear this, you kings! Listen, you rulers! I will sing to the LORD, I will sing; I will make music to the LORD, the God of Israel.*

**Judges 5:3**

---

## 4 SUNDAY

---

## 5 MONDAY
New Year's Resolution Week

*Set some short- and long-term goals for the year.*

## 6 TUESDAY
Epiphany

*The wise men arrive!*

## 7 WEDNESDAY

JANUARY
| S | M | T | W | T | F | S |
|---|---|---|---|---|---|---|
| | | | | 1 | 2 | 3 |
| 4 | 5 | 6 | 7 | 8 | 9 | 10 |
| 11 | 12 | 13 | 14 | 15 | 16 | 17 |
| 18 | 19 | 20 | 21 | 22 | 23 | 24 |
| 25 | 26 | 27 | 28 | 29 | 30 | 31 |

FEBRUARY
| S | M | T | W | T | F | S |
|---|---|---|---|---|---|---|
| 1 | 2 | 3 | 4 | 5 | 6 | 7 |
| 8 | 9 | 10 | 11 | 12 | 13 | 14 |
| 15 | 16 | 17 | 18 | 19 | 20 | 21 |
| 22 | 23 | 24 | 25 | 26 | 27 | 28 |
| 29 | | | | | | |

*Take a break! Brew a cup of tea and meditate on God's goodness.*

## 8 THURSDAY

## 9 FRIDAY

*Schedule eye appointment.*

## 10 SATURDAY

# January

**Prayer Requests**

**11** SUNDAY
**International Thank You Days**

*Write someone from your past or present who did something nice for you.*

**12** MONDAY

**13** TUESDAY

*Start a family music box: Fill it with bells, sticks, finger cymbals, shakers, kazoo, harmonica, triangle, drums, etc. Keep it handy for impromptu performances!*

# 14 WEDNESDAY

## JANUARY
S M T W T F S
1 2 3
4 5 6 7 8 9 10
11 12 13 14 15 16 17
18 19 20 21 22 23 24
25 26 27 28 29 30 31

## FEBRUARY
S M T W T F S
1 2 3 4 5 6 7
8 9 10 11 12 13 14
15 16 17 18 19 20 21
22 23 24 25 26 27 28
29

# 15 THURSDAY

# 16 FRIDAY
Religious Freedom Day

*Pray for our government leaders.*

# 17 SATURDAY

*Simmer a pot of your family's favorite soup tonight.*

# January

**Prayer Requests**

*Sing to him, sing praise to him; tell of all
his wonderful acts.*
*1 Chronicles 16:9*

---

**18** S U N D A Y
Sanctity of Life Sunday

---

**19** M O N D A Y
Martin Luther King Jr.'s Birthday Observed

---

**20** T U E S D A Y

# 21 WEDNESDAY
National Hugging Day

### JANUARY
| S | M | T | W | T | F | S |
|---|---|---|---|---|---|---|
|   |   |   |   | 1 | 2 | 3 |
| 4 | 5 | 6 | 7 | 8 | 9 | 10 |
| 11 | 12 | 13 | 14 | 15 | 16 | 17 |
| 18 | 19 | 20 | 21 | 22 | 23 | 24 |
| 25 | 26 | 27 | 28 | 29 | 30 | 31 |

### FEBRUARY
| S | M | T | W | T | F | S |
|---|---|---|---|---|---|---|
| 1 | 2 | 3 | 4 | 5 | 6 | 7 |
| 8 | 9 | 10 | 11 | 12 | 13 | 14 |
| 15 | 16 | 17 | 18 | 19 | 20 | 21 |
| 22 | 23 | 24 | 25 | 26 | 27 | 28 |
| 29 |   |   |   |   |   |   |

*A family hug is the best warmth on a chilly evening!*

# 22 THURSDAY

# 23 FRIDAY

# 24 SATURDAY
Healthy Weight Week

*Don't just think about it . . . get started!*

# January

**Prayer Requests**

*Sing to the LORD, all the earth; proclaim his salvation day after day.*
*1 Chronicles 16:23*

---

**25** SUNDAY
Super Bowl XXXVIII

*Chili dogs, coleslaw, and brownies make a great halftime meal!*

**26** MONDAY

---

**27** TUESDAY

# 28 WEDNESDAY

### JANUARY
| S | M | T | W | T | F | S |
|---|---|---|---|---|---|---|
|   |   |   |   | 1 | 2 | 3 |
| 4 | 5 | 6 | 7 | 8 | 9 | 10 |
| 11 | 12 | 13 | 14 | 15 | 16 | 17 |
| 18 | 19 | 20 | 21 | 22 | 23 | 24 |
| 25 | 26 | 27 | 28 | 29 | 30 | 31 |

### FEBRUARY
| S | M | T | W | T | F | S |
|---|---|---|---|---|---|---|
| 1 | 2 | 3 | 4 | 5 | 6 | 7 |
| 8 | 9 | 10 | 11 | 12 | 13 | 14 |
| 15 | 16 | 17 | 18 | 19 | 20 | 21 |
| 22 | 23 | 24 | 25 | 26 | 27 | 28 |
| 29 |   |   |   |   |   |   |

# 29 THURSDAY
**National Puzzle Day**

*Piece together a new puzzle.*

# 30 FRIDAY

*A good night for a family slumber party: games, popcorn, family videos, and hot chocolate!*

# 31 SATURDAY

# Run Lightly

When February rolls around, my husband, Ken, and I hit the road. Whether it's a conference or convention, you'll always recognize us by our luggage. Ken carries suitcases and hanging bags, heavy boxes for the motor and batteries of my wheelchair . . . and, oh, I can't forget the extra duffle for a few disability-related supplies. When our February travel schedule is in full swing, Ken knows he's got to stay in shape—he's not only lifting luggage, he has to lift me!

This is why he always packs his running shorts and shoes. If it's not pouring down rain, you can bet my husband will be jogging early in the morning before we head out to our first appointment. Even though we were in the midwest last week and the weather was icy cold, there was Ken, heading out the hotel door with shorts on. He looked funny wearing a hooded sweatshirt, scarf, gloves, and . . . nylon running shorts! I shouldn't have laughed. The best runners—the professional types—strip down to shorts in cold weather, too.

It's a good lesson. My "running instructions" are straight out of Hebrews 12:1. As we run the race, we're required to lay aside every sin or hindrance, every weight which might slow us down. The icy cold winds of adversity might tempt me to ease my pace, bundle up, and choose a more comfortable route, but God calls us to race with lives unburdened and unencumbered. Life is not a cake walk. We don't run the race for our glory; we run it for his—for the advancement of his kingdom, for the rescuing of lost souls, and for the rearing of godly families.

I've got a trip coming up the end of this month, and I know Ken and I will be packing for cold weather. It'll be sweaters and jackets . . . it'll also be nylon running shorts in his suitcase. It may be freezing out when Ken runs, but he is committed to lay aside any weight which might drag him down.

I would do well to do the same.

# February Planner

## Goals

American Heart Month
National Children's Dental Health Month
National Wild Bird Feeding Month

## Prayer Requests

## Bible Reading & Study

## People to See & Calls to Make

## Birthdays & Special Days

### Quote of the Month

Tune me, O Lord, into one harmony with thee, one full responsive vibrant chord: Unto thy praise, all love and melody, tune me, O Lord.

**Christina Rossetti**

# February 2004

| Sunday | Monday | Tuesday | Wednesday |
|---|---|---|---|
| 1 | 2 | 3 | 4 |
| 8 | 9 | 10 | 11 |
| 15 | 16<br>Presidents' Day | 17 | 18 |
| 22<br>Washington's Birthday | 23 | 24 | 25<br>Ash Wednesday |
| 29 | | | |

| Thursday | Friday | Saturday |
|---|---|---|
| 5 | 6 | 7 |
| 12<br>Lincoln's Birthday | 13 | 14<br>Valentine's Day |
| 19 | 20 | 21 |
| 26 | 27 | 28 |
| | | |

JANUARY

| S | M | T | W | T | F | S |
|---|---|---|---|---|---|---|
| | | | | | 1 | 2 | 3 |
| 4 | 5 | 6 | 7 | 8 | 9 | 10 |
| 11 | 12 | 13 | 14 | 15 | 16 | 17 |
| 18 | 19 | 20 | 21 | 22 | 23 | 24 |
| 25 | 26 | 27 | 28 | 29 | 30 | 31 |

MARCH

| S | M | T | W | T | F | S |
|---|---|---|---|---|---|---|
| | | 1 | 2 | 3 | 4 | 5 | 6 |
| 7 | 8 | 9 | 10 | 11 | 12 | 13 |
| 14 | 15 | 16 | 17 | 18 | 19 | 20 |
| 21 | 22 | 23 | 24 | 25 | 26 | 27 |
| 28 | 29 | 30 | 31 | | | |

# February

**Prayer Requests**

*Then the trees of the forest will sing, they will sing for joy before the LORD, for he comes to judge the earth. Give thanks to the LORD, for he is good; his love endures forever.*
*1 Chronicles 16:33–34*

---

**1** S U N D A Y

*Enjoy a drive (or sleigh ride!) after church today.*

---

**2** M O N D A Y
Groundhog Day

---

**3** T U E S D A Y

# 4 WEDNESDAY

FEBRUARY

| S | M | T | W | T | F | S |
|---|---|---|---|---|---|---|
| 1 | 2 | 3 | 4 | 5 | 6 | 7 |
| 8 | 9 | 10 | 11 | 12 | 13 | 14 |
| 15 | 16 | 17 | 18 | 19 | 20 | 21 |
| 22 | 23 | 24 | 25 | 26 | 27 | 28 |
| 29 | | | | | | |

MARCH

| S | M | T | W | T | F | S |
|---|---|---|---|---|---|---|
| | 1 | 2 | 3 | 4 | 5 | 6 |
| 7 | 8 | 9 | 10 | 11 | 12 | 13 |
| 14 | 15 | 16 | 17 | 18 | 19 | 20 |
| 21 | 22 | 23 | 24 | 25 | 26 | 27 |
| 28 | 29 | 30 | 31 | | | |

# 5 THURSDAY

*Don't forget to make those dental checkup appointments for your children.*

# 6 FRIDAY

*Full moon tonight: Bundle up and go for a moonlight stroll.*

# 7 SATURDAY

*Mail Valentine cards to folks who wouldn't expect one from you!*

# February

**Prayer Requests**

But let all who take refuge in you be glad; let them ever sing for joy. Spread your protection over them, that those who love your name may rejoice in you. For surely, O LORD, you bless the righteous; you surround them with your favor as with a shield.

*Psalm 5:11–12*

---

## 8 SUNDAY

*Have a family praise night for devotions.*

---

## 9 MONDAY

---

## 10 TUESDAY
**Bake for Family Fun Month**

*Enjoy baking old-fashioned, tried-and-true comfort foods this month.*

## 11 WEDNESDAY
**Thomas Edison's Birthday**

### FEBRUARY

| S | M | T | W | T | F | S |
|---|---|---|---|---|---|---|
|  | 1 | 2 | 3 | 4 | 5 | 6 | 7 |
| 8 | 9 | 10 | 11 | 12 | 13 | 14 |
| 15 | 16 | 17 | 18 | 19 | 20 | 21 |
| 22 | 23 | 24 | 25 | 26 | 27 | 28 |
| 29 |  |  |  |  |  |  |

### MARCH

| S | M | T | W | T | F | S |
|---|---|---|---|---|---|---|
|  | 1 | 2 | 3 | 4 | 5 | 6 |
| 7 | 8 | 9 | 10 | 11 | 12 | 13 |
| 14 | 15 | 16 | 17 | 18 | 19 | 20 |
| 21 | 22 | 23 | 24 | 25 | 26 | 27 |
| 28 | 29 | 30 | 31 |  |  |  |

*He said, "Genius is 1% inspiration and 99% perspiration."*

## 12 THURSDAY
**Abraham Lincoln's Birthday**

## 13 FRIDAY

## 14 SATURDAY
**Valentine's Day**

*A day to tell your special loved ones . . .*
*I LOVE YOU!!*

# February

**Prayer Requests**

---

## 15 SUNDAY

---

## 16 MONDAY

**Presidents' Day**

---

## 17 TUESDAY

*String popcorn, apples, cranberries, and balls of suet and hang on
a nearby tree branch for the birds.*

# 18 WEDNESDAY

**FEBRUARY**

| S | M | T | W | T | F | S |
|---|---|---|---|---|---|---|
| 1 | 2 | 3 | 4 | 5 | 6 | 7 |
| 8 | 9 | 10 | 11 | 12 | 13 | 14 |
| 15 | 16 | 17 | 18 | 19 | 20 | 21 |
| 22 | 23 | 24 | 25 | 26 | 27 | 28 |
| 29 | | | | | | |

**MARCH**

| S | M | T | W | T | F | S |
|---|---|---|---|---|---|---|
| | 1 | 2 | 3 | 4 | 5 | 6 |
| 7 | 8 | 9 | 10 | 11 | 12 | 13 |
| 14 | 15 | 16 | 17 | 18 | 19 | 20 |
| 21 | 22 | 23 | 24 | 25 | 26 | 27 |
| 28 | 29 | 30 | 31 | | | |

# 19 THURSDAY

# 20 FRIDAY
**Ansel Adams' Birthday**

*Spend some time enjoying the beautiful work of this American photographer.*

# 21 SATURDAY

*Prepare your heart for worship tomorrow.*

# February

**Prayer Requests**

*I will praise you, O LORD, with all my heart;*
*I will tell of all your wonders. I will be*
*glad and rejoice in you; I will sing praise to*
*your name, O Most High.*
*Psalm 9:1–2*

---

## 22 SUNDAY
George Washington's Birthday

*Sing hymns on your way to church this morning.*

---

## 23 MONDAY

---

## 24 TUESDAY
International Friendship Week

*Pray for Joni and Friends' "Wheels for the World" trips.*

## 25 WEDNESDAY
Ash Wednesday

### FEBRUARY
| S | M | T | W | T | F | S |
|---|---|---|---|---|---|---|
|   | 1 | 2 | 3 | 4 | 5 | 6 | 7 |
| 8 | 9 | 10 | 11 | 12 | 13 | 14 |
| 15 | 16 | 17 | 18 | 19 | 20 | 21 |
| 22 | 23 | 24 | 25 | 26 | 27 | 28 |
| 29 |

### MARCH
| S | M | T | W | T | F | S |
|---|---|---|---|---|---|---|
|   | 1 | 2 | 3 | 4 | 5 | 6 |
| 7 | 8 | 9 | 10 | 11 | 12 | 13 |
| 14 | 15 | 16 | 17 | 18 | 19 | 20 |
| 21 | 22 | 23 | 24 | 25 | 26 | 27 |
| 28 | 29 | 30 | 31 |

## 26 THURSDAY

## 27 FRIDAY
Henry Wadsworth Longfellow's Birthday

*Sit back, sip some flavored coffee, and read Longfellow's "The Song of Hiawatha."*

## 28 SATURDAY

*Take pictures of the winter birds who visit your homemade treats in the backyard.*

# Ears Up!

When the weather starts to feel like spring, I think back on blustery days when I would saddle up and enjoy horseback riding. That's probably why now, many years later, I take the road to work which passes by a horse show ring. Sometimes I pull over just to watch. Occasionally, there are several girls on their ponies, taking lessons from a riding instructor. But, this morning, I was almost breathless. . . .

The show ring was empty except for a woman astride a beautiful large bay gelding. The horse kept his head low and his neck arched. He didn't chomp at the bit to escape the reins, but simply trotted whenever the rider gave a little click-click. I delighted in the way he kept his ears up.

The way a horse keeps his ears up says a lot. The position of the ears shows a confident horse who is able to relax and focus on the path ahead. "Ears up" indicates a horse who is happy with the rider on his back.

I have learned so many lessons from observing horses. As I drove away from the show ring, I half-prayed, "Oh, Lord, help me to keep my ears up." I don't want to resist my Rider or chomp at the bit. I want to keep looking forward. And even if the path ahead is a complex maze of hurdles that he expects me to overcome, I know I can do it . . . I can do it as long as I feel his hand on me.

It's been more than 35 years since I've ridden horseback, but I can still hear the heavy breathing and the steady clip-clop of my horse's hooves. First Timothy 4:7 says, *"Train yourself to be godly."* That's good advice for anyone who wants to saddle up, lean into the bit, respond to the spur, keep the head low, and confidently move into the future with ears up! Train yourself to be godly. It's what Christians love to do when they trust the One who holds the reins.

# March Planner

## Goals

American Red Cross Month
National Craft Month
National Nutrition Month

## Prayer Requests

## Bible Reading & Study

## People to See & Calls to Make

## Birthdays & Special Days

## Quote of the Month

The human soul is a silent harp in God's choir whose strings need only to be swept by the divine breath to chime in with the harmonies of creation.
**Henry David Thoreau**

# *March* 2004

| Sunday | Monday | Tuesday | Wednesday |
|--------|--------|---------|-----------|
|        | 1      | 2       | 3         |
| 7      | 8      | 9       | 10        |
| 14     | 15     | 16      | 17<br>St. Patrick's Day |
| 21     | 22     | 23      | 24        |
| 28     | 29     | 30      | 31        |

| Thursday | Friday | Saturday |
|----------|--------|----------|
| 4 | 5 | 6 |
| 11 | 12 | 13 |
| 18 | 19 | 20<br>Spring Begins |
| 25 | 26 | 27 |
| | | |

# March

**Prayer Requests**

I will sing to the LORD, for he has been
good to me.
*Psalm 13:6*

---

**29** SUNDAY · *FEBRUARY*
**Leap Day**

---

**1** MONDAY · *MARCH*

---

**2** TUESDAY

**3** W E D N E S D A Y

**Help Someone See Month**

MARCH
S M T W T F S
1 2 3 4 5 6
7 8 9 10 11 12 13
14 15 16 17 18 19 20
21 22 23 24 25 26 27
28 29 30 31

APRIL
S M T W T F S
1 2 3
4 5 6 7 8 9 10
11 12 13 14 15 16 17
18 19 20 21 22 23 24
25 26 27 28 29 30

*Donate old eyeglasses for distribution to developing countries.*

**4** T H U R S D A Y

**5** F R I D A Y

**6** S A T U R D A Y

*Plant a row of sweet peas in your yard.*

# March

**Prayer Requests**

*Therefore I will praise you among the nations, O LORD; I will sing praises to your name.*

*Psalm 18:49*

---

**7** SUNDAY

---

**8** MONDAY

Commonwealth Day—United Kingdom

---

**9** TUESDAY

*Have all your W2's for tax preparation?*

# 10 WEDNESDAY

MARCH

| S | M | T | W | T | F | S |
|---|---|---|---|---|---|---|
| | 1 | 2 | 3 | 4 | 5 | 6 |
| 7 | 8 | 9 | 10 | 11 | 12 | 13 |
| 14 | 15 | 16 | 17 | 18 | 19 | 20 |
| 21 | 22 | 23 | 24 | 25 | 26 | 27 |
| 28 | 29 | 30 | 31 | | | |

APRIL

| S | M | T | W | T | F | S |
|---|---|---|---|---|---|---|
| | | | | 1 | 2 | 3 |
| 4 | 5 | 6 | 7 | 8 | 9 | 10 |
| 11 | 12 | 13 | 14 | 15 | 16 | 17 |
| 18 | 19 | 20 | 21 | 22 | 23 | 24 |
| 25 | 26 | 27 | 28 | 29 | 30 | |

# 11 THURSDAY
**Johnny Appleseed Day**

*He was a planter of orchards and friend of wild animals.*

# 12 FRIDAY

*Give a recorded book to a blind friend.*
*Call 1-800-638-1304.*

# 13 SATURDAY
**Genealogy Week**

*Start a new hobby: Begin the journey to knowing your heritage name by name, one ancestor at a time.*

# March

**Prayer Requests**

**14** SUNDAY

**15** MONDAY
**Deaf History Month**

**16** TUESDAY

*Make an appointment to donate blood.*

# 17 WEDNESDAY
St. Patrick's Day

MARCH

| S | M | T | W | T | F | S |
|---|---|---|---|---|---|---|
|   |   | 1 | 2 | 3 | 4 | 5 | 6 |
| 7 | 8 | 9 | 10 | 11 | 12 | 13 |
| 14 | 15 | 16 | 17 | 18 | 19 | 20 |
| 21 | 22 | 23 | 24 | 25 | 26 | 27 |
| 28 | 29 | 30 | 31 |   |   |   |

APRIL

| S | M | T | W | T | F | S |
|---|---|---|---|---|---|---|
|   |   |   |   | 1 | 2 | 3 |
| 4 | 5 | 6 | 7 | 8 | 9 | 10 |
| 11 | 12 | 13 | 14 | 15 | 16 | 17 |
| 18 | 19 | 20 | 21 | 22 | 23 | 24 |
| 25 | 26 | 27 | 28 | 29 | 30 |   |

*A hearty Irish stew might be the top of the order today!*

# 18 THURSDAY

# 19 FRIDAY

# 20 SATURDAY
Spring Begins

*Now's the time to plant that vegetable patch!*

# March

**Prayer Requests**

Then my head will be exalted above the
enemies who surround me; at his tabernacle
will I sacrifice with shouts of joy; I will sing
and make music to the LORD.
*Psalm 27:6*

---

## 21 SUNDAY

*Serve fried chicken, mashed potatoes, and creamed peas for
Sunday supper.*

---

## 22 MONDAY

---

## 23 TUESDAY
National Poison Prevention Week

*Update your home on safety against poisoning.*

# 24 WEDNESDAY

MARCH
S M T W T F S
1 2 3 4 5 6
7 8 9 10 11 12 13
14 15 16 17 18 19 20
21 22 23 24 25 26 27
28 29 30 31

APRIL
S M T W T F S
1 2 3
4 5 6 7 8 9 10
11 12 13 14 15 16 17
18 19 20 21 22 23 24
25 26 27 28 29 30

# 25 THURSDAY
**National Cleaning Week**

*A reminder to tackle spring cleaning:*
*Dedicate each day to a specific chore.*

# 26 FRIDAY

# 27 SATURDAY

*This is National Craft Month . . . how about*
*finishing up all those "half-started" projects!*

# March

**Prayer Requests**

You turned my wailing into dancing; you removed my sackcloth and clothed me with joy, that my heart may sing to you and not be silent. O LORD, my God, I will give you thanks forever.
*Psalm 30:11–12*

---

**28** SUNDAY

---

*Offer a ride to church to a disabled friend.*

**29** MONDAY

---

**30** TUESDAY

## 31 WEDNESDAY

MARCH

| S | M | T | W | T | F | S |
|---|---|---|---|---|---|---|
|   | 1 | 2 | 3 | 4 | 5 | 6 |
| 7 | 8 | 9 | 10 | 11 | 12 | 13 |
| 14 | 15 | 16 | 17 | 18 | 19 | 20 |
| 21 | 22 | 23 | 24 | 25 | 26 | 27 |
| 28 | 29 | 30 | 31 |   |   |   |

APRIL

| S | M | T | W | T | F | S |
|---|---|---|---|---|---|---|
|   |   |   |   | 1 | 2 | 3 |
| 4 | 5 | 6 | 7 | 8 | 9 | 10 |
| 11 | 12 | 13 | 14 | 15 | 16 | 17 |
| 18 | 19 | 20 | 21 | 22 | 23 | 24 |
| 25 | 26 | 27 | 28 | 29 | 30 |   |

## 1 THURSDAY · *APRIL*
**National Poetry Month**

*Take turns reading your favorite poem at dinner tonight.*

## 2 FRIDAY
**International Children's Book Day**

*Read about a missionary family.*

## 3 SATURDAY
**Daylight Savings Time Begins**

*Set your clocks forward one hour tonight.*

# A Surprise Ending

Remember the last time you watched your plans unravel and thought, *Lord, what's going on here?!* It happens to all of us. And it happened to our *Wheels for the World* team when they arrived in Poland to distribute wheelchairs and Bibles. Before the day had hardly started, their plans were in shreds. . . .

The distribution area was tiny. Then, before our team had a chance to set up, they turned and saw streams of hopeful disabled people and their families pouring through the doors of the distribution site. Our team was caught off guard.

Right away, the *Wheels* leader gathered the team to pray. Proverbs 19:21 was on their minds, *"Many are the plans in a man's heart, but it is the LORD's purpose that prevails."* Then they got to work. A tired father who had been carrying his five-year-old disabled boy finally reached the head of the line. He'd been waiting for hours and was excited that it was now his son's turn. But when he lifted him into the pre-assigned wheelchair—it didn't fit!

Our physical therapist ran back to the storeroom, pushed aside several adult wheelchairs, and reached for a child-sized one. It was the only one there. She was dismayed to see how highly customized it was—it had trunk supports from its original owner and the blue leather backing had "Jake" stitched across the middle.

When the family saw all the gizmos on it, they frowned. But the father lifted his son into the odd new chair. It fit *perfectly!* A circle of curious onlookers gathered around. "It's like it was made for him!" an interpreter exclaimed.

"By the way," one *Wheels* team member asked the boy's mother, "what is your son's name?"

"Jakob," she said matter-of-factly.

Yes, it was the perfect fit all the way down to the little boy's name. If you are struggling today with a plan-gone-haywire in your life, take heart from Jakob's story. Most of all, take comfort in Proverbs 19:21. The Lord's purpose *always* prevails. Just ask those happy parents in Poland!

# April Planner
## Goals

National Occupational Therapy Month
National Poetry Month
National Smile Month

## Prayer Requests

## Bible Reading & Study

## People to See & Calls to Make

## Birthdays & Special Days

### Quote of the Month

What is to reach the heart
must come from above; if it
does not come from thence,
it will be nothing but notes,
body without spirit.
**Ludwig van Beethoven**

# April 2004

| Sunday | Monday | Tuesday | Wednesday |
|--------|--------|---------|-----------|
|        |        |         |           |
| 4<br>Palm Sunday | 5 | 6<br>Passover | 7 |
| 11<br>Easter | 12 | 13 | 14 |
| 18 | 19 | 20 | 21 |
| 25 | 26 | 27 | 28 |

| Thursday | Friday | Saturday |
|---|---|---|
| 1 | 2 | 3 |
| 8 | 9<br>Good Friday | 10 |
| 15 | 16 | 17 |
| 22 | 23 | 24 |
| 29 | 30 | |

**MARCH**

| S | M | T | W | T | F | S |
|---|---|---|---|---|---|---|
| | | 1 | 2 | 3 | 4 | 5 | 6 |
| 7 | 8 | 9 | 10 | 11 | 12 | 13 |
| 14 | 15 | 16 | 17 | 18 | 19 | 20 |
| 21 | 22 | 23 | 24 | 25 | 26 | 27 |
| 28 | 29 | 30 | 31 | | | |

**MAY**

| S | M | T | W | T | F | S |
|---|---|---|---|---|---|---|
| | | | | | | 1 |
| 2 | 3 | 4 | 5 | 6 | 7 | 8 |
| 9 | 10 | 11 | 12 | 13 | 14 | 15 |
| 16 | 17 | 18 | 19 | 20 | 21 | 22 |
| 23 | 24 | 25 | 26 | 27 | 28 | 29 |
| 30 | 31 | | | | | |

# April

**Prayer Requests**

**4** SUNDAY
**Palm Sunday**

*Look up Matthew 21.*

**5** MONDAY

**6** TUESDAY
**Passover**

*Study about Passover in Exodus 12-13.*

# 7 WEDNESDAY

*Why not volunteer at a Joni and Friends Family Retreat? Call 1-818-707-5664 for information.*

### APRIL
| S | M | T | W | T | F | S |
|---|---|---|---|---|---|---|
|   |   |   |   | 1 | 2 | 3 |
| 4 | 5 | 6 | 7 | 8 | 9 | 10 |
| 11 | 12 | 13 | 14 | 15 | 16 | 17 |
| 18 | 19 | 20 | 21 | 22 | 23 | 24 |
| 25 | 26 | 27 | 28 | 29 | 30 |   |

### MAY
| S | M | T | W | T | F | S |
|---|---|---|---|---|---|---|
|   |   |   |   |   |   | 1 |
| 2 | 3 | 4 | 5 | 6 | 7 | 8 |
| 9 | 10 | 11 | 12 | 13 | 14 | 15 |
| 16 | 17 | 18 | 19 | 20 | 21 | 22 |
| 23 | 24 | 25 | 26 | 27 | 28 | 29 |
| 30 | 31 |   |   |   |   |   |

# 8 THURSDAY

# 9 FRIDAY
Good Friday

*Read passages about the Last Supper, Jesus' last words to his disciples, and Jesus' prayer for us in John 13–17.*

# 10 SATURDAY
National Kite Month

*Fly a kite at a park or beach this afternoon.*

# April

**Prayer Requests**

*For the word of the LORD is right and true;
he is faithful in all he does. The LORD loves
righteousness and justice; the earth is
full of his unfailing love.*
*Psalm 33:4–5*

---

**11** SUNDAY
Easter

*Look up the Easter story in Matthew 28 and share how your
life has been changed by it.*

**12** MONDAY
National Garden Week

*Start making your garden the prettiest in the neighborhood!*

**13** TUESDAY
Egg Salad Week

*Create a new way to use up those Easter eggs.*

## 14 WEDNESDAY

APRIL
| S | M | T | W | T | F | S |
|---|---|---|---|---|---|---|
|   |   |   |   | 1 | 2 | 3 |
| 4 | 5 | 6 | 7 | 8 | 9 | 10 |
| 11 | 12 | 13 | 14 | 15 | 16 | 17 |
| 18 | 19 | 20 | 21 | 22 | 23 | 24 |
| 25 | 26 | 27 | 28 | 29 | 30 |   |

MAY
| S | M | T | W | T | F | S |
|---|---|---|---|---|---|---|
|   |   |   |   |   |   | 1 |
| 2 | 3 | 4 | 5 | 6 | 7 | 8 |
| 9 | 10 | 11 | 12 | 13 | 14 | 15 |
| 16 | 17 | 18 | 19 | 20 | 21 | 22 |
| 23 | 24 | 25 | 26 | 27 | 28 | 29 |
| 30 | 31 |   |   |   |   |   |

*Order spring note cards from Joni and Friends;
just call 1-800-523-5777.*

## 15 THURSDAY

**Income Tax Day**

## 16 FRIDAY

## 17 SATURDAY

*Begin making vacation plans.*

# April

**Prayer Requests**

**18** S U N D A Y

**19** M O N D A Y
National Library Week

**20** T U E S D A Y
National Volunteer Week

*Your church needs more volunteers. Why not sign up?!*

## 21 WEDNESDAY
Queen Elizabeth II's Birthday—United Kingdom

APRIL

| S | M | T | W | T | F | S |
|---|---|---|---|---|---|---|
|   |   |   |   | 1 | 2 | 3 |
| 4 | 5 | 6 | 7 | 8 | 9 | 10 |
| 11 | 12 | 13 | 14 | 15 | 16 | 17 |
| 18 | 19 | 20 | 21 | 22 | 23 | 24 |
| 25 | 26 | 27 | 28 | 29 | 30 |   |

MAY

| S | M | T | W | T | F | S |
|---|---|---|---|---|---|---|
|   |   |   |   |   |   | 1 |
| 2 | 3 | 4 | 5 | 6 | 7 | 8 |
| 9 | 10 | 11 | 12 | 13 | 14 | 15 |
| 16 | 17 | 18 | 19 | 20 | 21 | 22 |
| 23 | 24 | 25 | 26 | 27 | 28 | 29 |
| 30 | 31 |   |   |   |   |   |

## 22 THURSDAY

## 23 FRIDAY

## 24 SATURDAY
National Wildlife Week

*Get a friend and go on a birdwatching hike.*

# April

**Prayer Requests**

---

## 25 SUNDAY
**Mother/Father Deaf Day**

*A day to honor deaf parents and recognize the gifts of culture and language they give to their hearing children.*

---

## 26 MONDAY

---

## 27 TUESDAY
National Occupational Therapy Month

*If you know any occupational therapists, give them a phone call and tell them how much they are appreciated.*

## 28 WEDNESDAY

### APRIL

| S | M | T | W | T | F | S |
|---|---|---|---|---|---|---|
|   |   |   |   | 1 | 2 | 3 |
| 4 | 5 | 6 | 7 | 8 | 9 | 10 |
| 11 | 12 | 13 | 14 | 15 | 16 | 17 |
| 18 | 19 | 20 | 21 | 22 | 23 | 24 |
| 25 | 26 | 27 | 28 | 29 | 30 |   |

### MAY

| S | M | T | W | T | F | S |
|---|---|---|---|---|---|---|
|   |   |   |   |   |   | 1 |
| 2 | 3 | 4 | 5 | 6 | 7 | 8 |
| 9 | 10 | 11 | 12 | 13 | 14 | 15 |
| 16 | 17 | 18 | 19 | 20 | 21 | 22 |
| 23 | 24 | 25 | 26 | 27 | 28 | 29 |
| 30 | 31 |   |   |   |   |   |

## 29 THURSDAY

## 30 FRIDAY
**National Honesty Day**

## 1 SATURDAY · *MAY*
**Mother Goose Day**

*Celebrate by reading nursery rhymes with a special child today.*

# Heart Melodies

May is here! Birds are singing and so am I. Anyone who spends time with me knows how much I enjoy singing. I don't pretend to hit all the right notes, but I sure do enjoy humming a hymn throughout the day. It struck me the other morning as I wheeled into work that there's hardly a time I enter the front door without a song on my lips. The other day it was . . .

*"In my heart there rings a melody, there rings a melody of heaven's harmony, in my heart there rings a melody, there rings a melody of love."* For me, that's not a sentimental Sunday school song. It's a fact of the Christian life. One of the key indicators that you're growing is the presence of a heaven-sent melody in your heart.

Ephesians 5:19 says, *"Make music in your heart to the Lord."* The heart is the core of your character, and what issues from it reveals who you really are. You can be sure that when you kick your mind out of gear and drop your intellectual defenses, you will do and say things by *heart*—you will reveal the "you" who you really are without even thinking about it. And what comes out of your heart? Hopefully, it'll be a melody from the Lord.

This is why I'm so grateful that hymns often come easily to mind (or I should say, heart). A scriptural song gives an undercurrent; it's the background to everything I do. A song on my lips tells me I'm changing, I'm growing, I'm maturing. The presence of a holy song in your life is a very basic and profound indicator of spiritual awareness.

As I see it, if the Lord rejoices over us with singing—and it says that in Zephaniah 3:17—if the Lord rejoices over us with a song, then *our* rejoicing over him should involve singing. So change the dial, tune in, and listen to God's song for you . . . then sing along in your heart . . . you and the Lord in stereo!

# May Planner

## Goals

National Arthritis Month
National Hamburger Month
Older Americans Month

## Prayer Requests

## Bible Reading & Study

## People to See & Calls to Make

## Birthdays & Special Days

### Quote of the Month

Who among us has not sought
peace in a song?

**Victor Hugo**

# *May* 2004

| Sunday | Monday | Tuesday | Wednesday |
|--------|--------|---------|-----------|
|        |        |         |           |
| 2 | 3 | 4 | 5 |
| 9<br>Mother's Day | 10 | 11 | 12 |
| 16 | 17 | 18 | 19 |
| 23 | 24 | 25 | 26 |
| 30 | 31<br>Memorial Day Observed | | |

| Thursday | Friday | Saturday |
|----------|--------|----------|
|  |  | 1 |
| 6<br>National Day of Prayer | 7 | 8 |
| 13 | 14 | 15<br>Armed Forces Day |
| 20 | 21 | 22 |
| 27 | 28 | 29 |

APRIL
S M T W T F S
1 2 3
4 5 6 7 8 9 10
11 12 13 14 15 16 17
18 19 20 21 22 23 24
25 26 27 28 29 30

JUNE
S M T W T F S
1 2 3 4 5
6 7 8 9 10 11 12
13 14 15 16 17 18 19
20 21 22 23 24 25 26
27 28 29 30

# May

**Prayer Requests**

*My heart is steadfast, O God, my heart is
steadfast; I will sing and make music.*
*Psalm 57:7*

---

**2** S U N D A Y
**National Family Week**

---

**3** M O N D A Y
**Be Kind to Animals Week**

*Give your pet a bath and a brushing.*

**4** T U E S D A Y

## 5 WEDNESDAY
**Teacher Appreciation Week**

MAY
S M T W T F S
1
2 3 4 5 6 7 8
9 10 11 12 13 14 15
16 17 18 19 20 21 22
23 24 25 26 27 28 29
30 31

JUNE
S M T W T F S
1 2 3 4 5
6 7 8 9 10 11 12
13 14 15 16 17 18 19
20 21 22 23 24 25 26
27 28 29 30

*Write or call a teacher who influenced your life.*

## 6 THURSDAY
**National Day of Prayer**

*Invite some friends over for a time of prayer.*

## 7 FRIDAY

## 8 SATURDAY
**National Nurses Week**

*A week to honor nurses everywhere who help to strengthen the health of our nation.*

# May

**Prayer Requests**

But I will sing of your strength, in the
morning I will sing of your love; for you are
my fortress, my refuge in times of trouble.
O my Strength, I sing praise to you; you,
O God, are my fortress, my loving God.
*Psalm 59:16–17*

---

**9** SUNDAY

Mother's Day

*A day to treat Mom to some much needed relaxation!*

---

**10** MONDAY

---

**11** TUESDAY

National Nursing Home Week

*Bake goodies and pass them out with a smile to shut-ins at your local nursing home.*

## 12 WEDNESDAY

### MAY
S M T W T F S
                    1
2 3 4 5 6 7 8
9 10 11 12 13 14 15
16 17 18 19 20 21 22
23 24 25 26 27 28 29
30 31

### JUNE
S M T W T F S
      1 2 3 4 5
6 7 8 9 10 11 12
13 14 15 16 17 18 19
20 21 22 23 24 25 26
27 28 29 30

## 13 THURSDAY
Police Week

*Take time this week to pray for the men and women
who risk their lives to protect us.*

## 14 FRIDAY
**Lewis & Clark Expedition Anniversary**

*Rent the "Lewis & Clark Expedition" video.*

## 15 SATURDAY
**Armed Forces Day**

*Send a letter to someone in military service.*

# May

**Prayer Requests**

Then will I ever sing praise to your name
and fulfill my vows day after day.
*Psalm 61:8*

---

**16** S U N D A Y
National Book Month

*Treat yourself to a unique pleasure: Read a good book.*

---

**17** M O N D A Y

---

**18** T U E S D A Y
National Family Month

*Time to take your annual family photo!*

# 19 WEDNESDAY

### MAY
| S | M | T | W | T | F | S |
|---|---|---|---|---|---|---|
|   |   |   |   |   |   | 1 |
| 2 | 3 | 4 | 5 | 6 | 7 | 8 |
| 9 | 10 | 11 | 12 | 13 | 14 | 15 |
| 16 | 17 | 18 | 19 | 20 | 21 | 22 |
| 23 | 24 | 25 | 26 | 27 | 28 | 29 |
| 30 | 31 |   |   |   |   |   |

### JUNE
| S | M | T | W | T | F | S |
|---|---|---|---|---|---|---|
|   |   | 1 | 2 | 3 | 4 | 5 |
| 6 | 7 | 8 | 9 | 10 | 11 | 12 |
| 13 | 14 | 15 | 16 | 17 | 18 | 19 |
| 20 | 21 | 22 | 23 | 24 | 25 | 26 |
| 27 | 28 | 29 | 30 |   |   |   |

# 20 THURSDAY
**Ascension Day**

# 21 FRIDAY

# 22 SATURDAY
**National Hamburger Month**

*Create your own double-decker burger for dinner.*

# May

**Prayer Requests**

---

## 23 SUNDAY
Older Americans Month

*Take an elderly neighbor to church and lunch today.*

---

## 24 MONDAY

---

## 25 TUESDAY

*How about a family fondue tonight?*

# 26 WEDNESDAY

MAY

| S | M | T | W | T | F | S |
|---|---|---|---|---|---|---|
|   |   |   |   |   |   | 1 |
| 2 | 3 | 4 | 5 | 6 | 7 | 8 |
| 9 | 10 | 11 | 12 | 13 | 14 | 15 |
| 16 | 17 | 18 | 19 | 20 | 21 | 22 |
| 23 | 24 | 25 | 26 | 27 | 28 | 29 |
| 30 | 31 |   |   |   |   |   |

JUNE

| S | M | T | W | T | F | S |
|---|---|---|---|---|---|---|
|   |   | 1 | 2 | 3 | 4 | 5 |
| 6 | 7 | 8 | 9 | 10 | 11 | 12 |
| 13 | 14 | 15 | 16 | 17 | 18 | 19 |
| 20 | 21 | 22 | 23 | 24 | 25 | 26 |
| 27 | 28 | 29 | 30 |   |   |   |

*Make a lunch date with your child—just the two of you!*

# 27 THURSDAY

# 28 FRIDAY

*Don't forget to shop for wedding gifts.*

# 29 SATURDAY
## National Bike Month

*Enjoy the spring weather . . . take a bike ride through the park.*

# Sharing the Burden

With the change of seasons, June is a good month to start something new. Maybe a garden, a cooking class, or how about joining a Bible study? I started attending one with my friend Charlene. She's a solid believer, firmly grounded in God's Word, mature . . . and scared. Charlene recently discovered she has multiple sclerosis. She can no longer drive to the store or read the labels of cans in her cupboard. That's why she enjoys this Bible study so much. Her heart becomes calm when she dives deep into the Bible.

Charlene and I usually sit next to each other. There's a good reason. I sit very tall in my wheelchair, and it's hard for me to lean over to read a book on someone's lap. But when my friend opens her giant-print Bible, I can easily see the super-large words.

Lately, though, I've had to read aloud for Charlene—her vision is beginning to deteriorate. It's heartbreaking. But the sadness is eased somewhat when she serves as my "hands" and I can be her "eyes." Because we are able to carry each other's burdens, as it says in Galatians 6:2, our limitations seem lighter.

Are you struggling with a burden today? Something that is choking your hopes and dreams for the future? Then take a little advice from a paralyzed person being led by the blind. When the hopeful lead the hurting, or the short lead the tall, or the poor lead the rich, or the old help the young—whatever the combo—remember that shared burdens ease the load. *And* multiply the joy.

Share your struggles today with someone for whom you can take on a burden, too. It'll take your eyes off your own load and—what do you know—your burdens will be halved and your joy will be doubled. All because you found someone whose needs were greater than your own. When it comes to Charlene and I, the blind *are* leading the paralyzed (or is it the other way around?). And praise the Lord, we're going somewhere!

# June Planner

Goals

National Iced Tea Month
National Rose Month

Prayer Requests

Bible Reading & Study

People to See & Calls to Make

Birthdays & Special Days

*Quote of the Month*

There's music in the dawning morn, there's music in the twilight cloud, there's music in the depth of night, when the world is still and dim, and the stars flame out in the pomp of light, like thrones of the cherubim!

**William Hone**

# June 2004

| Sunday | Monday | Tuesday | Wednesday |
|--------|--------|---------|-----------|
|        |        | 1       | 2         |
| 6      | 7      | 8       | 9         |
| 13     | 14<br>Flag Day | 15 | 16 |
| 20<br>Father's Day<br>Summer Begins | 21 | 22 | 23 |
| 27     | 28     | 29      | 30        |

| Thursday | Friday | Saturday |
|----------|--------|----------|
| 3 | 4 | 5 |
| 10 | 11 | 12 |
| 17 | 18 | 19 |
| 24 | 25 | 26 |
|  |  |  |

# June

**Prayer Requests**

The meadows are covered with flocks and
the valleys are mantled with grain; they
shout for joy and sing.
*Psalm 65:13*

---

**30** SUNDAY · *MAY*
Pentecost

*Read about Pentecost in the book of Acts.*

**31** MONDAY
**Memorial Day Observed**

*Pray for our servicemen and women.*

**1** TUESDAY · *JUNE*

*Why not serve with Joni and Friends' Wheels for
the World and help us distribute wheelchairs overseas?
Call 1-818-707-5664 for information.*

## 2 WEDNESDAY

### JUNE
| S | M | T | W | T | F | S |
|---|---|---|---|---|---|---|
|   |   | 1 | 2 | 3 | 4 | 5 |
| 6 | 7 | 8 | 9 | 10 | 11 | 12 |
| 13 | 14 | 15 | 16 | 17 | 18 | 19 |
| 20 | 21 | 22 | 23 | 24 | 25 | 26 |
| 27 | 28 | 29 | 30 |   |   |   |

### JULY
| S | M | T | W | T | F | S |
|---|---|---|---|---|---|---|
|   |   |   |   | 1 | 2 | 3 |
| 4 | 5 | 6 | 7 | 8 | 9 | 10 |
| 11 | 12 | 13 | 14 | 15 | 16 | 17 |
| 18 | 19 | 20 | 21 | 22 | 23 | 24 |
| 25 | 26 | 27 | 28 | 29 | 30 | 31 |

## 3 THURSDAY
Full Moon Tonight

## 4 FRIDAY

*On the last day of school, pick a handful of roses for your child's teacher.*

## 5 SATURDAY
National Family Day

*Drive to the waterside, have a picnic, and fly a kite together!*

# June

**Prayer Requests**

**6** SUNDAY
**Trinity Sunday**

**7** MONDAY

*Tell someone today about yesterday's sermon.*

**8** TUESDAY
**National Fishing Week**

# 9 WEDNESDAY

## JUNE
| S | M | T | W | T | F | S |
|---|---|---|---|---|---|---|
|   |   | 1 | 2 | 3 | 4 | 5 |
| 6 | 7 | 8 | 9 | 10 | 11 | 12 |
| 13 | 14 | 15 | 16 | 17 | 18 | 19 |
| 20 | 21 | 22 | 23 | 24 | 25 | 26 |
| 27 | 28 | 29 | 30 |   |   |   |

## JULY
| S | M | T | W | T | F | S |
|---|---|---|---|---|---|---|
|   |   |   |   | 1 | 2 | 3 |
| 4 | 5 | 6 | 7 | 8 | 9 | 10 |
| 11 | 12 | 13 | 14 | 15 | 16 | 17 |
| 18 | 19 | 20 | 21 | 22 | 23 | 24 |
| 25 | 26 | 27 | 28 | 29 | 30 | 31 |

*Pray for school graduates.*

# 10 THURSDAY

# 11 FRIDAY

*Give ice cream gift certificates to elementary school graduates.*

# 12 SATURDAY

# June

**Prayer Requests**

*May the nations be glad and sing for joy, for you rule the peoples justly and guide the nations of the earth.*

*Psalm 67:4*

---

**13** SUNDAY

Children's Day

---

**14** MONDAY

Flag Day

---

*Have a flag-raising ceremony with your family.*

**15** TUESDAY

# 16 WEDNESDAY

### JUNE
| S | M | T | W | T | F | S |
|---|---|---|---|---|---|---|
|   |   | 1 | 2 | 3 | 4 | 5 |
| 6 | 7 | 8 | 9 | 10 | 11 | 12 |
| 13 | 14 | 15 | 16 | 17 | 18 | 19 |
| 20 | 21 | 22 | 23 | 24 | 25 | 26 |
| 27 | 28 | 29 | 30 |   |   |   |

### JULY
| S | M | T | W | T | F | S |
|---|---|---|---|---|---|---|
|   |   |   |   | 1 | 2 | 3 |
| 4 | 5 | 6 | 7 | 8 | 9 | 10 |
| 11 | 12 | 13 | 14 | 15 | 16 | 17 |
| 18 | 19 | 20 | 21 | 22 | 23 | 24 |
| 25 | 26 | 27 | 28 | 29 | 30 | 31 |

*Encourage your child to start a "Summer Memory Box." All you need is a plain box with a lid. Your child can decorate it and fill it with fun summertime memories.*

# 17 THURSDAY

# 18 FRIDAY

*Sow some sunflowers for fall blooms.*

# 19 SATURDAY

*Do you know someone with a disability who needs a ride to church tomorrow?*

# June

**Prayer Requests**

Sing to God, sing praise to his name, extol
him who rides on the clouds—his name is
the LORD—and rejoice before him.

*Psalm 68:4*

---

**20** SUNDAY
Father's Day
Summer Begins

*Treat Dad to a day of relaxation!*

---

**21** MONDAY

---

**22** TUESDAY

## 23 WEDNESDAY
National Forgiveness Week

### JUNE
| S | M | T | W | T | F | S |
|---|---|---|---|---|---|---|
|   |   | 1 | 2 | 3 | 4 | 5 |
| 6 | 7 | 8 | 9 | 10 | 11 | 12 |
| 13 | 14 | 15 | 16 | 17 | 18 | 19 |
| 20 | 21 | 22 | 23 | 24 | 25 | 26 |
| 27 | 28 | 29 | 30 |   |   |   |

### JULY
| S | M | T | W | T | F | S |
|---|---|---|---|---|---|---|
|   |   |   |   | 1 | 2 | 3 |
| 4 | 5 | 6 | 7 | 8 | 9 | 10 |
| 11 | 12 | 13 | 14 | 15 | 16 | 17 |
| 18 | 19 | 20 | 21 | 22 | 23 | 24 |
| 25 | 26 | 27 | 28 | 29 | 30 | 31 |

## 24 THURSDAY
National Safety Month

*Stress safety around the pool.*

## 25 FRIDAY

## 26 SATURDAY

*Remember that vegetable patch you started in March? How about a "veggie" dinner!*

# June

**Prayer Requests**

I will sing of the LORD'S great love forever; with my mouth I will make your faithfulness known through all generations. I will declare that your love stands firm forever, that you established your faithfulness in heaven itself.
*Psalm 89:1–2*

## 27 SUNDAY

*Read the history of a familiar hymn as part of your family worship.*

## 28 MONDAY

## 29 TUESDAY
Deaf-Blindness Awareness Week

*A reminder to pray for those who are deaf and blind.*

## 30 WEDNESDAY

JUNE
S M T W T F S
1 2 3 4 5
6 7 8 9 10 11 12
13 14 15 16 17 18 19
20 21 22 23 24 25 26
27 28 29 30

JULY
S M T W T F S
1 2 3
4 5 6 7 8 9 10
11 12 13 14 15 16 17
18 19 20 21 22 23 24
25 26 27 28 29 30 31

## 1 THURSDAY · *JULY*
**Canada Day**

## 2 FRIDAY

*We're at the halfway point of 2004. How have you done on those resolutions?*

## 3 SATURDAY

*Know someone in a wheelchair? Offer to give it a polish and a shine.*

# Flags-a-Flyin'

In just a few weeks, the Summer Olympics will begin in Athens, Greece. Ken and I are hoping to catch the opening ceremonies on TV. I wonder if it'll match the last Winter Olympics held in Salt Lake City?

Do you remember what happened right before the opening fanfare, fireworks, and the marching in of the athletes? The lights dimmed, the music subsided, and then, under a soft spotlight, law enforcement officers and firefighters walked into the stadium holding the tattered and burned American flag pulled from the rubble of the World Trade Center. President Bush stood quietly . . . thousands of people placed their hands on their hearts . . . and you could have heard a pin drop. It was the most moving moment of the Winter Olympics.

During those Games, we witnessed the pride of American medalists as they stood on the podium. Many gold medalists gazed with tears in their eyes as the Stars and Stripes were raised to our National Anthem. (Pass the Kleenex!) My heart was gripped to watch their lips mouth the words to "The Star-Spangled Banner."

Ken and I were glued to the set. My eyes became wet every time the American flag was raised and I heard the drum roll introducing our National Anthem. And as it played, I always sang along. But I sang my favorite verse, the second one, which goes:

*And thus be it ever when free men shall stand between their loved homes and the war's desolation! Blest with vict'ry and peace, may the heav'n-rescued land Praise the Pow'r that hath made and preserved us a nation! Then conquer we must, when our cause it is just; And this be our motto: "In God is our trust!" And the star-spangled banner in triumph shall wave, O'er the land of the free and the home of the brave!*

There's joy in anticipating the Fourth of July and next month's Olympics. There's joy in praying for our country. There's peace as we "praise the Pow'r that hath made and preserved us a nation."

Happy July 4th everybody!

# July Planner

## Goals

National Hot Dog Month
National Ice Cream Month
National Recreation and Parks Month

## Prayer Requests

## Bible Reading & Study

## People to See & Calls to Make

## Birthdays & Special Days

### Quote of the Month

Next to theology I give to music the highest place and honor. Music is the art of the prophets, the only art that can calm the agitations of the soul; it is one of the most magnificent and delightful presents God has given us.

**Martin Luther**

# July *2004*

| Sunday | Monday | Tuesday | Wednesday |
|--------|--------|---------|-----------|
|        |        |         |           |
| 4<br>Independence Day | 5 | 6 | 7 |
| 11 | 12 | 13 | 14 |
| 18 | 19 | 20 | 21 |
| 25 | 26 | 27 | 28 |

| Thursday | Friday | Saturday |
|----------|--------|----------|
| 1 | 2 | 3 |
| 8 | 9 | 10 |
| 15 | 16 | 17 |
| 22 | 23 | 24 |
| 29 | 30 | 31 |

JUNE
S  M  T  W  T  F  S
         1  2  3  4  5
6  7  8  9  10 11 12
13 14 15 16 17 18 19
20 21 22 23 24 25 26
27 28 29 30

AUGUST
S  M  T  W  T  F  S
1  2  3  4  5  6  7
8  9  10 11 12 13 14
15 16 17 18 19 20 21
22 23 24 25 26 27 28
29 30 31

# July

**Prayer Requests**

**4** SUNDAY

Independence Day
Stephen Foster's Birthday

*Enjoy hot dogs and fireworks at a nearby park and sing some
of Foster's songs: "Oh! Susanna," "Camptown Races," and
"Swanee River."*

**5** MONDAY

P. T. Barnum's Birthday

*Make plans to attend a circus this summer.*

**6** TUESDAY

# 7 WEDNESDAY

### JULY

| S | M | T | W | T | F | S |
|---|---|---|---|---|---|---|
|   |   |   |   | 1 | 2 | 3 |
| 4 | 5 | 6 | 7 | 8 | 9 | 10 |
| 11 | 12 | 13 | 14 | 15 | 16 | 17 |
| 18 | 19 | 20 | 21 | 22 | 23 | 24 |
| 25 | 26 | 27 | 28 | 29 | 30 | 31 |

### AUGUST

| S | M | T | W | T | F | S |
|---|---|---|---|---|---|---|
| 1 | 2 | 3 | 4 | 5 | 6 | 7 |
| 8 | 9 | 10 | 11 | 12 | 13 | 14 |
| 15 | 16 | 17 | 18 | 19 | 20 | 21 |
| 22 | 23 | 24 | 25 | 26 | 27 | 28 |
| 29 | 30 | 31 |   |   |   |   |

*Pray with a friend on the phone today.*

# 8 THURSDAY

# 9 FRIDAY

*This weekend, offer some help to a family caring for an elderly member.*

# 10 SATURDAY

# July

**Prayer Requests**

It is good to praise the LORD and make music to your name, O Most High, to proclaim your love in the morning and your faithfulness at night, to the music of the ten-stringed lyre and the melody of the harp.

*Psalm 92:1–3*

---

## 11 SUNDAY
E. B. White's Birthday

*This afternoon, lie in the shade and read one of E. B. White's books for fun: "Charlotte's Web," "Stuart Little," or "The Trumpet of the Swan."*

---

## 12 MONDAY

*Freeze bananas for a cool summer treat.*

---

## 13 TUESDAY

# 14 WEDNESDAY

**JULY**

| S | M | T | W | T | F | S |
|---|---|---|---|---|---|---|
| | | | | 1 | 2 | 3 |
| 4 | 5 | 6 | 7 | 8 | 9 | 10 |
| 11 | 12 | 13 | 14 | 15 | 16 | 17 |
| 18 | 19 | 20 | 21 | 22 | 23 | 24 |
| 25 | 26 | 27 | 28 | 29 | 30 | 31 |

**AUGUST**

| S | M | T | W | T | F | S |
|---|---|---|---|---|---|---|
| 1 | 2 | 3 | 4 | 5 | 6 | 7 |
| 8 | 9 | 10 | 11 | 12 | 13 | 14 |
| 15 | 16 | 17 | 18 | 19 | 20 | 21 |
| 22 | 23 | 24 | 25 | 26 | 27 | 28 |
| 29 | 30 | 31 | | | | |

*Have a family praise night for devotions.*

# 15 THURSDAY

# 16 FRIDAY

# 17 SATURDAY

*Plan a bike-hike through the park.*

# July

**Prayer Requests**

For you make me glad by your deeds, O
LORD; I sing for joy at the works of your
hands. How great are your works, O LORD,
how profound your thoughts!

*Psalm 92:4–5*

---

## 18 SUNDAY

**National Ice Cream Day**

*Dish up "Sunday" sundaes for dessert.*

---

## 19 MONDAY

---

## 20 TUESDAY

*Plan a light summertime dinner of hors d'oeuvres.*

# 21 WEDNESDAY

JULY

S  M  T  W  T  F  S
            1  2  3
4  5  6  7  8  9  10
11 12 13 14 15 16 17
18 19 20 21 22 23 24
25 26 27 28 29 30 31

AUGUST

S  M  T  W  T  F  S
1  2  3  4  5  6  7
8  9  10 11 12 13 14
15 16 17 18 19 20 21
22 23 24 25 26 27 28
29 30 31

# 22 THURSDAY

*Set out a pitcher of iced tea to welcome home the gang.*

# 23 FRIDAY

# 24 SATURDAY

**Cousins Day**

*Celebrate family ties by inviting all the relatives to a potluck cookout or a field day.*

## July
**Prayer Requests**

*Come, let us sing for joy to the LORD; let us shout aloud to the Rock of our salvation.*
*Psalm 95:1*

**25** SUNDAY
Parents' Day

**26** MONDAY
National Salad Week

*Visit a farmers' market and pick out fresh ingredients to toss into a grand supper salad.*

**27** TUESDAY

# 28 WEDNESDAY

JULY

S M T W T F S
          1  2  3
4  5  6  7  8  9  10
11 12 13 14 15 16 17
18 19 20 21 22 23 24
25 26 27 28 29 30 31

AUGUST

S M T W T F S
1  2  3  4  5  6  7
8  9  10 11 12 13 14
15 16 17 18 19 20 21
22 23 24 25 26 27 28
29 30 31

*Gaze at the stars tonight . . . see if you can pick out your favorite summer constellation.*

# 29 THURSDAY

# 30 FRIDAY

*Have an overnight camp-out at the lake or seashore.*

# 31 SATURDAY

*Ask a person who lives alone out to lunch after church tomorrow.*

# The Sparrow Makes the Point

Summertime is the perfect time for trips to the zoo. I was just a little girl when my parents took me to the Baltimore Zoo, but I shall never forget the aviary. It was a large bird exhibition, and it was a-flutter with every kind of squawking, brightly colored, feathery creature you could imagine. There were zany big parrots, funny-looking toucans, stern eagles, and know-it-all owls. I had never seen such an array of wonderful, noisy wildlife.

My mother pointed out an interesting feature about the bird exhibition. She showed me the little sparrows fluttering in and out of all the cages, making their homes in the rafters. They didn't seem to be important enough to be put in a cage with the other birds. They weren't worth admiring, and they didn't warrant a plaque that explained their name in Latin or where they came from. Their pictures didn't appear in the guide book. Virtually everybody touring the aviary was completely unaware of their presence.

I felt sorry for the little birds. But my mother remarked that—aha!—unlike the parrots and toucans in the cages (some of them had little shackles on their legs with chains tethering them), the sparrows were free. They were free to go and do as they pleased.

My mom also reminded me that Jesus didn't speak about flamingoes, but he did speak about sparrows. And he used them to underscore an important lesson about trusting God. *"Do not be afraid, little flock,"* Jesus said to his fearful disciples, *"for your Father has been pleased to give you the kingdom"* (Luke 12:32). Could it be that the Lord was not talking about a flock of sheep, but a flock of birds? Maybe little birds?

Friend, if you're assaulted by worries today, remember this: If God has given you the Kingdom (which he has) then he's given you *everything*. You're free in him! And if the Lord concerns himself with a rag-tag sparrow, he cares about everything that concerns you. And you can take *that* to the aviary.

# August Planner

## Goals

National Back-to-School Month
Family Fun Month

## Prayer Requests

## Bible Reading & Study

## People to See & Calls to Make

## Birthdays & Special Days

### Quote of the Month

Music is the language spoken
by angels.

**Henry Wadsworth
Longfellow**

# *August* 2004

| Sunday | Monday | Tuesday | Wednesday |
|--------|--------|---------|-----------|
| 1 | 2<br>Friendship Day | 3 | 4 |
| 8 | 9 | 10 | 11 |
| 15 | 16 | 17 | 18 |
| 22 | 23 | 24 | 25 |
| 29 | 30 | 31 | |

| Thursday | Friday | Saturday |
|----------|--------|----------|
| 5 | 6 | 7 |
| 12 | 13 | 14 |
| 19 | 20 | 21 |
| 26 | 27 | 28 |
|  |  |  |

JULY

| S | M | T | W | T | F | S |
|---|---|---|---|---|---|---|
|  |  |  |  | 1 | 2 | 3 |
| 4 | 5 | 6 | 7 | 8 | 9 | 10 |
| 11 | 12 | 13 | 14 | 15 | 16 | 17 |
| 18 | 19 | 20 | 21 | 22 | 23 | 24 |
| 25 | 26 | 27 | 28 | 29 | 30 | 31 |

SEPTEMBER

| S | M | T | W | T | F | S |
|---|---|---|---|---|---|---|
|  |  |  | 1 | 2 | 3 | 4 |
| 5 | 6 | 7 | 8 | 9 | 10 | 11 |
| 12 | 13 | 14 | 15 | 16 | 17 | 18 |
| 19 | 20 | 21 | 22 | 23 | 24 | 25 |
| 26 | 27 | 28 | 29 | 30 |  |  |

# August

**Prayer Requests**

Let us come before him with thanksgiving and extol him with music and song. For the LORD is the great God, the great King above all gods.

*Psalm 95:2–3*

---

## 1 SUNDAY
**Sisters' Day**

*Send a card not only to your sister, but to a sister-in-law, sorority sister, or Christian sister.*

---

## 2 MONDAY
**Friendship Day**

*Surprise a friend with a fresh-baked peach cobbler.*

---

## 3 TUESDAY

*Plan a summertime dinner of hand-picked fresh vegetables.*

**4** WEDNESDAY
**National Smile Week**

AUGUST
S M T W T F S
1 2 3 4 5 6 7
8 9 10 11 12 13 14
15 16 17 18 19 20 21
22 23 24 25 26 27 28
29 30 31

SEPTEMBER
S M T W T F S
1 2 3 4
5 6 7 8 9 10 11
12 13 14 15 16 17 18
19 20 21 22 23 24 25
26 27 28 29 30

*Share a smile and it will come back to you.*

**5** THURSDAY

**6** FRIDAY

**7** SATURDAY

*Build your own birdbath: Place a terra-cotta saucer on top of an inverted clay pot. Put in your garden and fill with water.*

# August

**Prayer Requests**

Sing to the LORD a new song; sing to the
LORD, all the earth. Sing to the LORD, praise
his name; proclaim his salvation day after day.
*Psalm 96:1–2*

---

**8** SUNDAY

---

*Pack an evening picnic at the lake—including candles.*

**9** MONDAY

---

**10** TUESDAY

## 11 WEDNESDAY
National Back-to-School Month

AUGUST
S M T W T F S
1 2 3 4 5 6 7
8 9 10 11 12 13 14
15 16 17 18 19 20 21
22 23 24 25 26 27 28
29 30 31

SEPTEMBER
S M T W T F S
1 2 3 4
5 6 7 8 9 10 11
12 13 14 15 16 17 18
19 20 21 22 23 24 25
26 27 28 29 30

*Begin helping your child fill his school backpack with supplies.*

## 12 THURSDAY

## 13 FRIDAY
Annie Oakley's Birthday

*Look up her biography on the Internet.*

## 14 SATURDAY

*Plan a day trip to the mountains.*

# August

**Prayer Requests**

---

## 15 SUNDAY
National Friendship Week

*A week to focus on friendships: yourself on Sunday, spouse on Monday, children on Tuesday, family on Wednesday, friends on Thursday, co-workers on Friday, and neighbors on Saturday.*

## 16 MONDAY

---

## 17 TUESDAY
Davy Crockett's Birthday

*Spend time this month researching American frontiersmen.*

# 18 WEDNESDAY

## AUGUST

| S | M | T | W | T | F | S |
|---|---|---|---|---|---|---|
| | 1 | 2 | 3 | 4 | 5 | 6 | 7 |
| 8 | 9 | 10 | 11 | 12 | 13 | 14 |
| 15 | 16 | 17 | 18 | 19 | 20 | 21 |
| 22 | 23 | 24 | 25 | 26 | 27 | 28 |
| 29 | 30 | 31 | | | | |

## SEPTEMBER

| S | M | T | W | T | F | S |
|---|---|---|---|---|---|---|
| | | | | 1 | 2 | 3 | 4 |
| 5 | 6 | 7 | 8 | 9 | 10 | 11 |
| 12 | 13 | 14 | 15 | 16 | 17 | 18 |
| 19 | 20 | 21 | 22 | 23 | 24 | 25 |
| 26 | 27 | 28 | 29 | 30 | | |

# 19 THURSDAY
**National Forgiveness Day**

*A day to focus on forgiving others.*

# 20 FRIDAY

# 21 SATURDAY

*Roast marshmallows over a campfire and then watch for shooting stars—don't forget to make a wish!*

# August

**Prayer Requests**

I will sing of your love and justice; to you,
O LORD, I will sing praise.
*Psalm 101:1*

---

**22** SUNDAY
Be an Angel Day

*Be a blessing in someone's life: Take an older family member on a drive through the countryside.*

---

**23** MONDAY

---

**24** TUESDAY

*Freeze fruit juice popsicles for the neighborhood kids.*

# 25 WEDNESDAY

### AUGUST
| S | M | T | W | T | F | S |
|---|---|---|---|---|---|---|
| 1 | 2 | 3 | 4 | 5 | 6 | 7 |
| 8 | 9 | 10 | 11 | 12 | 13 | 14 |
| 15 | 16 | 17 | 18 | 19 | 20 | 21 |
| 22 | 23 | 24 | 25 | 26 | 27 | 28 |
| 29 | 30 | 31 | | | | |

### SEPTEMBER
| S | M | T | W | T | F | S |
|---|---|---|---|---|---|---|
| | | | 1 | 2 | 3 | 4 |
| 5 | 6 | 7 | 8 | 9 | 10 | 11 |
| 12 | 13 | 14 | 15 | 16 | 17 | 18 |
| 19 | 20 | 21 | 22 | 23 | 24 | 25 |
| 26 | 27 | 28 | 29 | 30 | | |

*Time to sign up for a fall Bible study.*

# 26 THURSDAY

# 27 FRIDAY

*Make a family bulletin board. Add drawings, photos, chore lists, invitations, and important phone numbers.*

# 28 SATURDAY

# August

**Prayer Requests**

*I will sing to the LORD all my life; I will sing praise to my God as long as I live. May my meditation be pleasing to him, as I rejoice in the LORD.*
*Psalm 104:33–34*

---

## 29 SUNDAY

*Invite friends over for an old-fashioned songfest tonight.*

---

## 30 MONDAY

---

## 31 TUESDAY

*Pray for your child's (or grandchild's) new school teacher.*

# 1 WEDNESDAY · *SEPTEMBER*

Baby Safety Month

AUGUST

| S | M | T | W | T | F | S |
|---|---|---|---|---|---|---|
| 1 | 2 | 3 | 4 | 5 | 6 | 7 |
| 8 | 9 | 10 | 11 | 12 | 13 | 14 |
| 15 | 16 | 17 | 18 | 19 | 20 | 21 |
| 22 | 23 | 24 | 25 | 26 | 27 | 28 |
| 29 | 30 | 31 | | | | |

SEPTEMBER

| S | M | T | W | T | F | S |
|---|---|---|---|---|---|---|
| | | | 1 | 2 | 3 | 4 |
| 5 | 6 | 7 | 8 | 9 | 10 | 11 |
| 12 | 13 | 14 | 15 | 16 | 17 | 18 |
| 19 | 20 | 21 | 22 | 23 | 24 | 25 |
| 26 | 27 | 28 | 29 | 30 | | |

# 2 THURSDAY

# 3 FRIDAY

National Waffle Week

*Serve waffle and egg sandwiches for dinner.*

# 4 SATURDAY

*Clean and pack away summer clothes.*

# Serving God on the Subway

My friend Glenda is a Mennonite who tends a small farm in the beautiful green hills of Lancaster County, Pennsylvania. You'll never see her without her small white cap, whether hoeing her garden or scattering grain for her chickens.

Glenda is an active member in her church choir. Shortly after the terrorist attacks of September 11th in 2001, she and her choir friends—most of whom live on small farms—wondered, *How can we help the people in New York City?*

God gave them a wonderful idea. Early one morning, two weeks after the attacks, they boarded the bus and headed for New York City, taking with them a stack of cassettes of their favorite hymns. During the three-hour drive to the city, they prayed and sang all the way.

When they crossed the Hudson River and arrived downtown, their bus stopped at the first subway station. Glenda and her friends disembarked—they looked quite a sight in their simple farming clothes. But even in the hustle of the city, amidst honking horns and heavy traffic, they weren't daunted. They collected their music and marched down the steep steps to the subway station.

At the bottom, they huddled against a cool, concrete wall. They knew the high ceiling would provide the perfect setting. After they prayed—and while people were rushing by—they took a deep breath and began a four-part harmony of "Rock of Ages."

Suddenly stockbrokers slowed their pace. Students exiting the subway to run to class paused. Shoppers heading for Park Avenue and part-time actors running to 42nd Street hesitated. All turned their heads to listen to the farmers from the cornfields of Lancaster County—and as they paused to listen, Glenda gave away the cassettes.

There is *always* a way to share the love of Christ. There's always a fresh way to give Christian encouragement. Opportunities abound when it comes to reaching out and loving people to Jesus. Just ask Glenda. Just ask one of those stockbrokers or students who, that day, wiped a tear from their eyes.

# September Planner

Goals

## Prayer Requests

## Bible Reading & Study

## People to See & Calls to Make

## Birthdays & Special Days

### Quote of the Month

God is the organist, we are His instruments, His Spirit sounds each pipe and gives the tone of its strength.

**Angelus Silesius**

# September 2004

| Sunday | Monday | Tuesday | Wednesday |
|---|---|---|---|
| | | | 1 |
| 5 | 6<br>Labor Day | 7 | 8 |
| 12<br>Grandparent's Day | 13 | 14 | 15 |
| 19 | 20 | 21 | 22<br>Autumn Begins |
| 26 | 27 | 28 | 29 |

| Thursday | Friday | Saturday |
|----------|--------|----------|
| 2 | 3 | 4 |
| 9 | 10 | 11 |
| 16<br>Rosh Hashanah | 17 | 18 |
| 23 | 24 | 25<br>Yom Kippur |
| 30 | | |

AUGUST

| S | M | T | W | T | F | S |
|---|---|---|---|---|---|---|
| 1 | 2 | 3 | 4 | 5 | 6 | 7 |
| 8 | 9 | 10 | 11 | 12 | 13 | 14 |
| 15 | 16 | 17 | 18 | 19 | 20 | 21 |
| 22 | 23 | 24 | 25 | 26 | 27 | 28 |
| 29 | 30 | 31 | | | | |

OCTOBER

| S | M | T | W | T | F | S |
|---|---|---|---|---|---|---|
| | | | | | 1 | 2 |
| 3 | 4 | 5 | 6 | 7 | 8 | 9 |
| 10 | 11 | 12 | 13 | 14 | 15 | 16 |
| 17 | 18 | 19 | 20 | 21 | 22 | 23 |
| 24 | 25 | 26 | 27 | 28 | 29 | 30 |
| 31 | | | | | | |

# September

**Prayer Requests**

Sing to him, sing praise to him; tell of all his wonderful acts. Glory in his holy name; let the hearts of those who seek the LORD rejoice.

*Psalm 105:2–3*

---

## 5 SUNDAY

*Sing favorite hymns on the way to church today.*

---

## 6 MONDAY
**Labor Day—United States and Canada**

---

## 7 TUESDAY
**National Sewing Month**

*Begin a needle project to give to a loved one at Christmas.*

## 8 WEDNESDAY

### SEPTEMBER
| S | M | T | W | T | F | S |
|---|---|---|---|---|---|---|
|   |   |   | 1 | 2 | 3 | 4 |
| 5 | 6 | 7 | 8 | 9 | 10 | 11 |
| 12 | 13 | 14 | 15 | 16 | 17 | 18 |
| 19 | 20 | 21 | 22 | 23 | 24 | 25 |
| 26 | 27 | 28 | 29 | 30 |   |   |

### OCTOBER
| S | M | T | W | T | F | S |
|---|---|---|---|---|---|---|
|   |   |   |   |   | 1 | 2 |
| 3 | 4 | 5 | 6 | 7 | 8 | 9 |
| 10 | 11 | 12 | 13 | 14 | 15 | 16 |
| 17 | 18 | 19 | 20 | 21 | 22 | 23 |
| 24 | 25 | 26 | 27 | 28 | 29 | 30 |
| 31 |   |   |   |   |   |   |

## 9 THURSDAY
**National Honey Month**

*Do a research project on honeybees and beekeepers.*

## 10 FRIDAY

## 11 SATURDAY

*Spend the day at the county fair.*

# September

**Prayer Requests**

*My heart is steadfast, O God; I will sing and make music with all my soul. Awake, harp and lyre! I will awaken the dawn.*
*Psalm 108:1–2*

---

**12** SUNDAY
**National Grandparent's Day**

*Remember to call or visit and tell them you love them; it'll make their day!*

---

**13** MONDAY

---

**14** TUESDAY

# 15 WEDNESDAY

**SEPTEMBER**

| S | M | T | W | T | F | S |
|---|---|---|---|---|---|---|
|   |   |   | 1 | 2 | 3 | 4 |
| 5 | 6 | 7 | 8 | 9 | 10 | 11 |
| 12 | 13 | 14 | 15 | 16 | 17 | 18 |
| 19 | 20 | 21 | 22 | 23 | 24 | 25 |
| 26 | 27 | 28 | 29 | 30 |   |   |

**OCTOBER**

| S | M | T | W | T | F | S |
|---|---|---|---|---|---|---|
|   |   |   |   |   | 1 | 2 |
| 3 | 4 | 5 | 6 | 7 | 8 | 9 |
| 10 | 11 | 12 | 13 | 14 | 15 | 16 |
| 17 | 18 | 19 | 20 | 21 | 22 | 23 |
| 24 | 25 | 26 | 27 | 28 | 29 | 30 |
| 31 |   |   |   |   |   |   |

*Make appointments for your children's eye and health exams.*

# 16 THURSDAY
Rosh Hashanah

# 17 FRIDAY
Constitution Week

*Do you know your Bill of Rights?*

# 18 SATURDAY

*For beautiful spring flowers, plant crocus, daffodil, hyacinth, paperwhite, and tulip bulbs now.*

# September

**Prayer Requests**

Sing to the LORD with thanksgiving;
make music to our God on the harp.

*Psalm 147:7*

---

**19** S U N D A Y

---

**20** M O N D A Y
National Rehabilitation Awareness Celebration

*Salute dedicated healthcare professionals.*

---

**21** T U E S D A Y
Religious Freedom Week

## 22 WEDNESDAY
Autumn Begins

### SEPTEMBER
| S | M | T | W | T | F | S |
|---|---|---|---|---|---|---|
|   |   |   |   | 1 | 2 | 3 | 4 |
| 5 | 6 | 7 | 8 | 9 | 10 | 11 |
| 12 | 13 | 14 | 15 | 16 | 17 | 18 |
| 19 | 20 | 21 | 22 | 23 | 24 | 25 |
| 26 | 27 | 28 | 29 | 30 |   |   |

### OCTOBER
| S | M | T | W | T | F | S |
|---|---|---|---|---|---|---|
|   |   |   |   |   | 1 | 2 |
| 3 | 4 | 5 | 6 | 7 | 8 | 9 |
| 10 | 11 | 12 | 13 | 14 | 15 | 16 |
| 17 | 18 | 19 | 20 | 21 | 22 | 23 |
| 24 | 25 | 26 | 27 | 28 | 29 | 30 |
| 31 |   |   |   |   |   |   |

*Arrange a flower centerpiece and use a pumpkin for a vase.*

## 23 THURSDAY
Deaf Awareness Week

## 24 FRIDAY

*Visit an apple festival in your area.*

## 25 SATURDAY
Yom Kippur

# September

**Prayer Requests**

---

**26** SUNDAY
National Good Neighbor Day

*Arrange a neighborhood potluck block party.*

---

**27** MONDAY

---

**28** TUESDAY

*Send Christmas presents to your church's missionaries.*

## 29 WEDNESDAY

SEPTEMBER
S M T W T F S
1 2 3 4
5 6 7 8 9 10 11
12 13 14 15 16 17 18
19 20 21 22 23 24 25
26 27 28 29 30

OCTOBER
S M T W T F S
1 2
3 4 5 6 7 8 9
10 11 12 13 14 15 16
17 18 19 20 21 22 23
24 25 26 27 28 29 30
31

*Invite a new friend or family member to Bible study and prayer meeting tonight.*

## 30 THURSDAY

## 1 FRIDAY · OCTOBER
**National Disability Employment Awareness Month**

*Call the Job Accommodation Network at 1-800-526-7234.*

## 2 SATURDAY
**National Cookie Month**

*Ask family members to take turns baking their favorite cookie this month.*

# That Feels Like Me!

Whenever I wash my hair, I park in front of my sink, lean forward, and let my girlfriend, Dana, "go at it" as she stands to my side and lathers my hair. Last week, when she had almost finished, she asked, "Would you like me to wash your face while you're under the faucet?"

"Sure," I gurgled. When she began using her fingers to wash around my eyes, I gasped. "Oh, oh . . ." I tried to explain what I was feeling, but I couldn't. All I could say was, "That feels like me!"

While Dana was massaging my face, it felt as though her hands were *mine*. She was rubbing my face *exactly* the way I used to with my hands. When Dana patted my face and hair dry, she also had to press the towel against my eyes. I was crying. But they weren't tears of sadness. They were tears of joy about the future. "This was a reminder that soon—and very soon," I said, "I'll be able to wash my own face with new, glorified hands!"

As I wheeled into the day with a fresh hairdo, I also rejoiced in my fresh perspective on heaven. Maybe there was a time when I would have sighed, "Aw, I wish I were back in the old days when I could wash my own face!" But now I say, "Wow, *this* is the way it will soon be. Heaven is coming. I'll have glorified hands!" In the long run, I haven't lost anything over the last three decades. I've gained. I've gained a happy dependence on God and a joy over the smallest of pleasures—even the pleasure of washing my face.

Memories now push me joyfully into the future rather than pull me somberly back into the past. Because I'm a Christian, the future has a happy, magnetic pull on my heart. That's something I can rejoice in every time I wash my face! That's something I will rejoice in this month when I celebrate another year down . . . another year closer to heaven.

# October Planner

## Goals

National Cookie Month
National Crime Prevention Month
National Disability Employment Awareness Month

## Prayer Requests

## Bible Reading & Study

## People to See & Calls to Make

## Birthdays & Special Days

# *October* 2004

| Sunday | Monday | Tuesday | Wednesday |
|---|---|---|---|
| | | | |
| 3 | 4 | 5 | 6 |
| 10 | 11 Columbus Day Observed | 12 | 13 |
| 17 | 18 | 19 | 20 |
| 24 Mother-in-Law Day | 25 | 26 | 27 |
| 31 | | | |

| Thursday | Friday | Saturday |
|----------|--------|----------|
|  | 1 | 2 |
| 7 | 8 | 9 |
| 14 | 15 | 16<br>Boss Day<br>Sweetest Day |
| 21 | 22 | 23 |
| 28 | 29 | 30 |

SEPTEMBER
S M T W T F S
· 1 2 3 4
5 6 7 8 9 10 11
12 13 14 15 16 17 18
19 20 21 22 23 24 25
26 27 28 29 30

NOVEMBER
S M T W T F S
1 2 3 4 5 6
7 8 9 10 11 12 13
14 15 16 17 18 19 20
21 22 23 24 25 26 27
28 29 30

# October

*An evil man is snared by his own sin, but a righteous one can sing and be glad.*
*Proverbs 29:6*

---

## 3 SUNDAY
**Fire Prevention Week**

*Contact your local fire station and ask them how you can update your home in fire safety.*

## 4 MONDAY
**Child Health Day**

*Take your children for a checkup.*

## 5 TUESDAY

# 6 WEDNESDAY

OCTOBER

| S | M | T | W | T | F | S |
|---|---|---|---|---|---|---|
|   |   |   |   |   | 1 | 2 |
| 3 | 4 | 5 | 6 | 7 | 8 | 9 |
| 10 | 11 | 12 | 13 | 14 | 15 | 16 |
| 17 | 18 | 19 | 20 | 21 | 22 | 23 |
| 24 | 25 | 26 | 27 | 28 | 29 | 30 |
| 31 |   |   |   |   |   |   |

NOVEMBER

| S | M | T | W | T | F | S |
|---|---|---|---|---|---|---|
|   | 1 | 2 | 3 | 4 | 5 | 6 |
| 7 | 8 | 9 | 10 | 11 | 12 | 13 |
| 14 | 15 | 16 | 17 | 18 | 19 | 20 |
| 21 | 22 | 23 | 24 | 25 | 26 | 27 |
| 28 | 29 | 30 |   |   |   |   |

*Check batteries in your smoke alarm.*

# 7 THURSDAY

# 8 FRIDAY

# 9 SATURDAY

*Decorate your front porch with pumpkins, gourds, hay bales, pots of mums, and sunflowers.*

# October

Sing to the LORD, for he has done glorious
things; let this be known to all the world.
Shout aloud and sing for joy, people of Zion,
for great is the Holy One of Israel among you.
*Isaiah 12:5–6*

---

**10** SUNDAY

---

**11** MONDAY
Columbus Day Observed
Thanksgiving Day—Canada

---

**12** TUESDAY
National School Lunch Week

*Surprise your child with sandwiches cut into shapes with cookie
cutters and a crunchy veggie caterpillar: Slide cucumber slices
onto a straw and finish with a cherry tomato head!*

# 13 WEDNESDAY

OCTOBER
S M T W T F S
1 2
3 4 5 6 7 8 9
10 11 12 13 14 15 16
17 18 19 20 21 22 23
24 25 26 27 28 29 30
31

NOVEMBER
S M T W T F S
1 2 3 4 5 6
7 8 9 10 11 12 13
14 15 16 17 18 19 20
21 22 23 24 25 26 27
28 29 30

# 14 THURSDAY

# 15 FRIDAY
White Cane Safety Day

*Job opportunities for the blind: 1-800-638-7518.*

# 16 SATURDAY
Boss Day
Sweetest Day

*Enjoy the fall weather by taking a walk and then come home to a freshly baked berry pie.*

# October

**Prayer Requests**

---

**17** SUNDAY
National Sunday School Teacher Appreciation Day

*Remember your Sunday school teacher today with a word of encouragement.*

---

**18** MONDAY

---

**19** TUESDAY

## 20 WEDNESDAY

OCTOBER

| S | M | T | W | T | F | S |
|---|---|---|---|---|---|---|
|   |   |   |   |   | 1 | 2 |
| 3 | 4 | 5 | 6 | 7 | 8 | 9 |
| 10 | 11 | 12 | 13 | 14 | 15 | 16 |
| 17 | 18 | 19 | 20 | 21 | 22 | 23 |
| 24 | 25 | 26 | 27 | 28 | 29 | 30 |
| 31 |   |   |   |   |   |   |

NOVEMBER

| S | M | T | W | T | F | S |
|---|---|---|---|---|---|---|
|   | 1 | 2 | 3 | 4 | 5 | 6 |
| 7 | 8 | 9 | 10 | 11 | 12 | 13 |
| 14 | 15 | 16 | 17 | 18 | 19 | 20 |
| 21 | 22 | 23 | 24 | 25 | 26 | 27 |
| 28 | 29 | 30 |   |   |   |   |

*Talk to a businessperson at your church about hiring the disabled.*

## 21 THURSDAY

*Roast the seeds from the sunflowers you planted last summer.*

## 22 FRIDAY

## 23 SATURDAY

*Invite some friends over for a pumpkin carving contest and enjoy hot spiced cider and apple cake for dessert.*

# October

**Prayer Requests**

## 24 SUNDAY
United Nations Day
Mother-in-Law Day

*. . . or is it Mother-in-Love Day?*

## 25 MONDAY

## 26 TUESDAY
National Popcorn Poppin' Month

*Invite friends for table games and some favorite flavored popcorn.*

# 27 WEDNESDAY

### OCTOBER
| S | M | T | W | T | F | S |
|---|---|---|---|---|---|---|
|   |   |   |   |   | 1 | 2 |
| 3 | 4 | 5 | 6 | 7 | 8 | 9 |
| 10 | 11 | 12 | 13 | 14 | 15 | 16 |
| 17 | 18 | 19 | 20 | 21 | 22 | 23 |
| 24 | 25 | 26 | 27 | 28 | 29 | 30 |
| 31 |   |   |   |   |   |   |

### NOVEMBER
| S | M | T | W | T | F | S |
|---|---|---|---|---|---|---|
|   | 1 | 2 | 3 | 4 | 5 | 6 |
| 7 | 8 | 9 | 10 | 11 | 12 | 13 |
| 14 | 15 | 16 | 17 | 18 | 19 | 20 |
| 21 | 22 | 23 | 24 | 25 | 26 | 27 |
| 28 | 29 | 30 |   |   |   |   |

*Look at the full moon tonight and remember to reflect God's love to others.*

# 28 THURSDAY
**Statue of Liberty Dedication Anniversary (1886)**

*"Give me your tired, your poor, your huddled masses yearning to breathe free, the wretched refuse of your teeming shore. Send these, the homeless, tempest-tost to me, I lift my lamp beside the golden door."*
Sonnet by Emma Lazarus on the base of the Statue of Liberty

# 29 FRIDAY

# 30 SATURDAY
**Daylight Savings Time Ends**

*Turn clocks back one hour tonight.*

# Living Water

When November weather becomes icy and rainy, I love to escape for a day or two to the little town of Palm Desert. Recently I had to be there for a conference, and during a break several friends and I drove outside of town to take the tram to the top of Mt. San Jacinto, one of the highest mountains in southern California. We knew the views from the top would be spectacular.

As the tram began climbing, the scenery became breathtaking. On one side you could see the sprawling Mojave Desert. On the other, the craggy face of the mountain. We passed massive rocks and cliffs. Everything looked bone dry. Yet right below us was a long, twisting line of green trees and shrubbery. The snow from the top of Mt. San Jacinto (yes, this desert mountain is so high, in November it has snow at the top) was melting and trickling down the crevice. All along the crevice, there was *green*.

I was stunned at the clear demarcation between the greenery and the dry ground. It wasn't as though the grass spread out and became thin until the desert took over. Rather, the green just . . . stopped. Along the edge of the creek were life and vitality . . . a half-inch to the left was dead, hard dirt.

I stared at that tiny line of green life winding its way up the mountain, weaving in and out, around and under the rocks. I kept thinking, *That's like my life in Christ*. If I miss a day communing with the Savior, if I skip a few hours speaking or singing about him, I become *dry*. The truth is, we can't spread thin our spirituality. We can't survive on yesterday's Living Water. Life in Christ is a daily thing. It's a green thing!

Jesus said in John 7:38, *"Whoever believes in me, as the Scripture has said, streams of living water will flow from within him."* Stay green . . . and stay growing . . . stay near the Living Water. Because the Savior is no tiny trickle. He's the river of life.

# November Planner

## Goals

Family Stories Month
National Family Caregivers Month
National Hospice Month

## Prayer Requests

## Bible Reading & Study

## People to See & Calls to Make

## Birthdays & Special Days

### Quote of the Month

Music is almost all we have of
heaven on earth.

**Joseph Addison**

# November *2004*

| Sunday | Monday | Tuesday | Wednesday |
|---|---|---|---|
| | 1 | 2<br>Election Day | 3 |
| 7 | 8 | 9 | 10 |
| 14 | 15 | 16 | 17 |
| 21 | 22 | 23 | 24 |
| 28<br>First Sunday of Advent | 29 | 30 | |

| Thursday | Friday | Saturday |
|---|---|---|
| 4 | 5 | 6 |
| 11<br>Veterans Day | 12 | 13 |
| 18 | 19 | 20 |
| 25<br>Thanksgiving | 26 | 27 |
| | | |

# November

**Prayer Requests**

*Sing to the LORD a new song, his praise from the ends of the earth, you who go down to the sea, and all that is in it, you islands, and all who live in them.*

*Isaiah 42:10*

---

**31** SUNDAY · *OCTOBER*

---

*Take a Sunday drive after church services.*

---

**1** MONDAY · *NOVEMBER*
National Authors' Day

---

*Read a book this month by your favorite American author, perhaps Mark Twain's "The Prince and the Pauper."*

---

**2** TUESDAY
General Election Day

---

*Pray for local, state, and national leaders and ... Vote!*

# 3 WEDNESDAY

**NOVEMBER**

| S | M | T | W | T | F | S |
|---|---|---|---|---|---|---|
| | 1 | 2 | 3 | 4 | 5 | 6 |
| 7 | 8 | 9 | 10 | 11 | 12 | 13 |
| 14 | 15 | 16 | 17 | 18 | 19 | 20 |
| 21 | 22 | 23 | 24 | 25 | 26 | 27 |
| 28 | 29 | 30 | | | | |

**DECEMBER**

| S | M | T | W | T | F | S |
|---|---|---|---|---|---|---|
| | | | 1 | 2 | 3 | 4 |
| 5 | 6 | 7 | 8 | 9 | 10 | 11 |
| 12 | 13 | 14 | 15 | 16 | 17 | 18 |
| 19 | 20 | 21 | 22 | 23 | 24 | 25 |
| 26 | 27 | 28 | 29 | 30 | 31 | |

*Order Christmas cards from Joni and Friends.*

# 4 THURSDAY

# 5 FRIDAY

# 6 SATURDAY
**John Philip Sousa's Birthday**

*Strike up the band with a CD of "The Stars and Stripes Forever."*

# November

The LORD your God is with you, he is mighty
to save. He will take great delight in you, he
will quiet you with his love, he will rejoice
over you with singing.
*Zephaniah 3:17*

---

**7** S U N D A Y

---

**8** M O N D A Y

*Wildlife fun: Make a garland of orange and apple wedges,
peanuts in the shell, cranberries, and popcorn. Wrap around an
evergreen wreath and hang outside.*

---

**9** T U E S D A Y

## 10 WEDNESDAY
**Martin Luther's Birthday**

NOVEMBER
S M T W T F S
1 2 3 4 5 6
7 8 9 10 11 12 13
14 15 16 17 18 19 20
21 22 23 24 25 26 27
28 29 30

DECEMBER
S M T W T F S
1 2 3 4
5 6 7 8 9 10 11
12 13 14 15 16 17 18
19 20 21 22 23 24 25
26 27 28 29 30 31

*Read a biography of Luther, the leader of the Protestant Reformation.*

## 11 THURSDAY
**Veterans Day**
**Remembrance Day—Canada**

*Pray for our servicemen and women.*

## 12 FRIDAY

*How about sending a Thanksgiving family newsletter?*

## 13 SATURDAY

# November

**Prayer Requests**

About midnight Paul and Silas were praying
and singing hymns to God, and the other
prisoners were listening to them.

*Acts 16:25*

---

**14** S U N D A Y

---

*Visit a museum or art gallery this afternoon.*

**15** M O N D A Y

---

**16** T U E S D A Y
National Children's Book Week

# 17 WEDNESDAY
**American Education Week**

NOVEMBER
S M T W T F S
1 2 3 4 5 6
7 8 9 10 11 12 13
14 15 16 17 18 19 20
21 22 23 24 25 26 27
28 29 30

DECEMBER
S M T W T F S
1 2 3 4
5 6 7 8 9 10 11
12 13 14 15 16 17 18
19 20 21 22 23 24 25
26 27 28 29 30 31

*Do you know all the state governors?*

# 18 THURSDAY

# 19 FRIDAY

*Order your turkey for Thanksgiving dinner.*

# 20 SATURDAY

*Make that phone call today that you've been putting off. Write that letter that you've not gotten around to writing. You'll feel better!*

# November

**Prayer Requests**

---

**21** SUNDAY
National Bible Week

*Give a Bible to a non-Christian friend.*

---

**22** MONDAY

---

**23** TUESDAY
National Game and Puzzle Week

*Learn a new game you've never played before.*

# 24 WEDNESDAY

**NOVEMBER**

| S | M | T | W | T | F | S |
|---|---|---|---|---|---|---|
|   | 1 | 2 | 3 | 4 | 5 | 6 |
| 7 | 8 | 9 | 10 | 11 | 12 | 13 |
| 14 | 15 | 16 | 17 | 18 | 19 | 20 |
| 21 | 22 | 23 | 24 | 25 | 26 | 27 |
| 28 | 29 | 30 |   |   |   |   |

**DECEMBER**

| S | M | T | W | T | F | S |
|---|---|---|---|---|---|---|
|   |   |   | 1 | 2 | 3 | 4 |
| 5 | 6 | 7 | 8 | 9 | 10 | 11 |
| 12 | 13 | 14 | 15 | 16 | 17 | 18 |
| 19 | 20 | 21 | 22 | 23 | 24 | 25 |
| 26 | 27 | 28 | 29 | 30 | 31 |   |

*Write a verse of praise on the inside of your Thanksgiving dinner place cards.*

# 25 THURSDAY
**Thanksgiving Day**

*Take turns sharing your verse of praise.*

# 26 FRIDAY

*Make turkey BLT's from your leftovers.*

# 27 SATURDAY

# November

**Prayer Requests**

---

**28** SUNDAY
First Sunday in Advent

*Put up an Advent calendar.*

---

**29** MONDAY
Louisa May Alcott's Birthday

*Re-read the American classic "Little Women."*

---

**30** TUESDAY

# 1 WEDNESDAY · DECEMBER

**Cookie Cutter Week**

NOVEMBER

| S | M | T | W | T | F | S |
|---|---|---|---|---|---|---|
| | | 1 | 2 | 3 | 4 | 5 | 6 |
| 7 | 8 | 9 | 10 | 11 | 12 | 13 |
| 14 | 15 | 16 | 17 | 18 | 19 | 20 |
| 21 | 22 | 23 | 24 | 25 | 26 | 27 |
| 28 | 29 | 30 | | | | |

DECEMBER

| S | M | T | W | T | F | S |
|---|---|---|---|---|---|---|
| | | | 1 | 2 | 3 | 4 |
| 5 | 6 | 7 | 8 | 9 | 10 | 11 |
| 12 | 13 | 14 | 15 | 16 | 17 | 18 |
| 19 | 20 | 21 | 22 | 23 | 24 | 25 |
| 26 | 27 | 28 | 29 | 30 | 31 | |

*Use your holiday cookie cutters: Bake and decorate sugar cookies.*

# 2 THURSDAY

*Offer to do Christmas shopping for a disabled friend.*

# 3 FRIDAY

# 4 SATURDAY

*Dedicate this afternoon to addressing Christmas cards.*

# A Christmas Healing

It was 1968 and Christmas was around the corner. I was still new to my wheelchair and feeling sad. There was one thing I could still do—sing. Diana, my friend from school choir, rounded up a few friends for a sing-a-long. It was nearly Christmas Eve and we decided to go caroling. Someone suggested we drive down to the old railway station in Baltimore. "The acoustics would be great!"

We weren't disappointed. The station was nearly empty at that late hour. When our little group finished the last glorious note of "Joy to the World," we listened to it echo off the high ceiling. A few sailors applauded. We were a hit.

Suddenly a uniformed guard appeared. "Okay, enough of this. This isn't a Christmas party," he said gruffly. "This is a place of business. You young people clear out."

"Aw, really?" Diana whined in fun.

The guard didn't think she was funny. "And you . . . ," he pointed at me in my wheelchair. "You put that back where you found it!"

This was too funny to be true. "Sir, I wish I *could* get out of it, but I can't. It's mine."

"Don't you sass me. It belongs here, now put it back!"

"Honestly, I'm paralyzed. I really am!" I said, trying to keep a straight face.

All of a sudden he turned red. "Okay, just get out of here," he said. My friends threw me in Diana's car and we sped home, singing loudly all the way. To be sitting head-level with my friends, to wind down the car windows and let the icy night air waft the laughter and music, to play so happily that no sad thought could possibly enter my head, was *heavenly*.

It was also a gift. No, I didn't get healed that Christmas of 1968, but . . . almost. At least in the eyes of a guard in a railway station. And as I lay in bed that night, full of the joy that only great fellowship can bring, I realized God had given me the best Christmas gift of all . . .

Contentment.

# December Planner

Goals

Jesus' Birthday
_____

Prayer Requests


_____

Bible Reading & Study


_____

People to See & Calls to Make


_____

Birthdays & Special Days

## Quote of the Month

Music is God's best gift to man, the only art of heaven given to earth, the only art of earth we take to heaven.

**Letitia Elizabeth Landon**

# December 2004

| Sunday | Monday | Tuesday | Wednesday |
|--------|--------|---------|-----------|
|        |        |         | 1 |
| 5 | 6 | 7 | 8<br>First Day of Hanukkah |
| 12 | 13 | 14 | 15 |
| 19 | 20 | 21<br>Winter Begins | 22 |
| 26 | 27 | 28 | 29 |

| Thursday | Friday | Saturday |
|----------|--------|----------|
| 2 | 3 | 4 |
| 9 | 10 | 11 |
| 16 | 17 | 18 |
| 23 | 24<br>Christmas Eve | 25<br>Christmas Day |
| 30 | 31 | |

**NOVEMBER**

| S | M | T | W | T | F | S |
|---|---|---|---|---|---|---|
| | 1 | 2 | 3 | 4 | 5 | 6 |
| 7 | 8 | 9 | 10 | 11 | 12 | 13 |
| 14 | 15 | 16 | 17 | 18 | 19 | 20 |
| 21 | 22 | 23 | 24 | 25 | 26 | 27 |
| 28 | 29 | 30 | | | | |

**JANUARY 2005**

| S | M | T | W | T | F | S |
|---|---|---|---|---|---|---|
| | | | | | | 1 |
| 2 | 3 | 4 | 5 | 6 | 7 | 8 |
| 9 | 10 | 11 | 12 | 13 | 14 | 15 |
| 16 | 17 | 18 | 19 | 20 | 21 | 22 |
| 23 | 24 | 25 | 26 | 27 | 28 | 29 |
| 30 | 31 | | | | | |

# December

**Prayer Requests**

**5** SUNDAY

*Spread a picnic by the fireplace tonight—complete with blanket and candles.*

**6** MONDAY

*Family Project: Start baking and decorating a beautiful gingerbread village to enjoy through the Christmas holidays.*

**7** TUESDAY

**8** WEDNESDAY
**First Day of Hanukkah**

DECEMBER

| S | M | T | W | T | F | S |
|---|---|---|---|---|---|---|
|   |   |   | 1 | 2 | 3 | 4 |
| 5 | 6 | 7 | 8 | 9 | 10 | 11 |
| 12 | 13 | 14 | 15 | 16 | 17 | 18 |
| 19 | 20 | 21 | 22 | 23 | 24 | 25 |
| 26 | 27 | 28 | 29 | 30 | 31 |   |

JANUARY 2005

| S | M | T | W | T | F | S |
|---|---|---|---|---|---|---|
|   |   |   |   |   |   | 1 |
| 2 | 3 | 4 | 5 | 6 | 7 | 8 |
| 9 | 10 | 11 | 12 | 13 | 14 | 15 |
| 16 | 17 | 18 | 19 | 20 | 21 | 22 |
| 23 | 24 | 25 | 26 | 27 | 28 | 29 |
| 30 | 31 |   |   |   |   |   |

*Send your Jewish friends Hanukkah cards.*

**9** THURSDAY

*Make your nativity scene come alive: Since the wise men are now starting their journey, place them and their camels in another room . . .*

**10** FRIDAY

*Each day through the month, move the wise men closer on their journey to the nativity scene.*

**11** SATURDAY

*Take a walk through the neighborhood and enjoy the lights.*

# December

**Prayer Requests**

*Let the word of Christ dwell in you richly as yo
teach and admonish one another with all wisdon
and as you sing psalms, hymns and spiritual song
with gratitude in your hearts to God.*
*Colossians 3:16*

---

**12** S U N D A Y

*Invite someone who is alone to celebrate the decorating and festivities; they often could use a cheery celebration.*

---

**13** M O N D A Y

---

**14** T U E S D A Y

*Wrap gifts early.*

# 15 WEDNESDAY
Bill of Rights Day

DECEMBER
S M T W T F S
            1  2  3  4
5  6  7  8  9 10 11
12 13 14 15 16 17 18
19 20 21 22 23 24 25
26 27 28 29 30 31

JANUARY 2005
S M T W T F S
                  1
2  3  4  5  6  7  8
9 10 11 12 13 14 15
16 17 18 19 20 21 22
23 24 25 26 27 28 29
30 31

# 16 THURSDAY

*Each evening at mealtime, pray for the people who've sent you Christmas cards.*

# 17 FRIDAY

*Go caroling through the neighborhood.*

# 18 SATURDAY

*Have a "Happy Birthday Jesus" party— complete with a cake!*

# December

**Prayer Requests**

**19** SUNDAY

*This evening, light candles and enjoy listening to
a recording of Handel's "Messiah."*

**20** MONDAY
**Sacagawea's Death Anniversary**

*She was an interpreter for Lewis and Clark. Look up her
biography on the Internet.*

**21** TUESDAY
**Winter Begins**

*Celebrate with hot chocolate and a favorite Christmas story.*

## 22 WEDNESDAY

**DECEMBER**

| S | M | T | W | T | F | S |
|---|---|---|---|---|---|---|
|   |   |   | 1 | 2 | 3 | 4 |
| 5 | 6 | 7 | 8 | 9 | 10 | 11 |
| 12 | 13 | 14 | 15 | 16 | 17 | 18 |
| 19 | 20 | 21 | 22 | 23 | 24 | 25 |
| 26 | 27 | 28 | 29 | 30 | 31 |   |

**JANUARY 2005**

| S | M | T | W | T | F | S |
|---|---|---|---|---|---|---|
|   |   |   |   |   |   | 1 |
| 2 | 3 | 4 | 5 | 6 | 7 | 8 |
| 9 | 10 | 11 | 12 | 13 | 14 | 15 |
| 16 | 17 | 18 | 19 | 20 | 21 | 22 |
| 23 | 24 | 25 | 26 | 27 | 28 | 29 |
| 30 | 31 |   |   |   |   |   |

## 23 THURSDAY

## 24 FRIDAY
Christmas Eve

*Attend a candlelight service this evening.*

## 25 SATURDAY
Christmas Day

*Read the Christmas story from the Bible before opening gifts.*

# December

**Prayer Requests**

Then I heard every creature in heaven and on
earth and under the earth and on the sea, and
all that is in them, singing: "To him who sits
on the throne and to the Lamb be praise and
honor and glory and power, for ever and ever!"
*Revelation 5:13*

---

**26** SUNDAY
Boxing Day—Canada and United Kingdom

---

**27** MONDAY

*Thanks for sharing the year with me.*

**28** TUESDAY

*Choose a Bible verse for 2005.*

# 29 WEDNESDAY

### DECEMBER
S M T W T F S
            1  2  3  4
5  6  7  8  9  10 11
12 13 14 15 16 17 18
19 20 21 22 23 24 25
26 27 28 29 30 31

### JANUARY 2005
S M T W T F S
                  1
2  3  4  5  6  7  8
9  10 11 12 13 14 15
16 17 18 19 20 21 22
23 24 25 26 27 28 29
30 31

# 30 THURSDAY

# 31 FRIDAY
**New Year's Eve**
**Make Up Your Mind Day**

*Round up the family and make resolutions together.*

# 1 SATURDAY · *JANUARY*
**New Year's Day 2005**

*Make it a goal to read your Bible through this year.*

# 2004

## JANUARY
| S | M | T | W | T | F | S |
|---|---|---|---|---|---|---|
|   |   |   |   | 1 | 2 | 3 |
| 4 | 5 | 6 | 7 | 8 | 9 | 10 |
| 11 | 12 | 13 | 14 | 15 | 16 | 17 |
| 18 | 19 | 20 | 21 | 22 | 23 | 24 |
| 25 | 26 | 27 | 28 | 29 | 30 | 31 |

## FEBRUARY
| S | M | T | W | T | F | S |
|---|---|---|---|---|---|---|
| 1 | 2 | 3 | 4 | 5 | 6 | 7 |
| 8 | 9 | 10 | 11 | 12 | 13 | 14 |
| 15 | 16 | 17 | 18 | 19 | 20 | 21 |
| 22 | 23 | 24 | 25 | 26 | 27 | 28 |
| 29 |   |   |   |   |   |   |

## MARCH
| S | M | T | W | T | F | S |
|---|---|---|---|---|---|---|
|   | 1 | 2 | 3 | 4 | 5 | 6 |
| 7 | 8 | 9 | 10 | 11 | 12 | 13 |
| 14 | 15 | 16 | 17 | 18 | 19 | 20 |
| 21 | 22 | 23 | 24 | 25 | 26 | 27 |
| 28 | 29 | 30 | 31 |   |   |   |

## APRIL
| S | M | T | W | T | F | S |
|---|---|---|---|---|---|---|
|   |   |   |   | 1 | 2 | 3 |
| 4 | 5 | 6 | 7 | 8 | 9 | 10 |
| 11 | 12 | 13 | 14 | 15 | 16 | 17 |
| 18 | 19 | 20 | 21 | 22 | 23 | 24 |
| 25 | 26 | 27 | 28 | 29 | 30 |   |

## MAY
| S | M | T | W | T | F | S |
|---|---|---|---|---|---|---|
|   |   |   |   |   |   | 1 |
| 2 | 3 | 4 | 5 | 6 | 7 | 8 |
| 9 | 10 | 11 | 12 | 13 | 14 | 15 |
| 16 | 17 | 18 | 19 | 20 | 21 | 22 |
| 23 | 24 | 25 | 26 | 27 | 28 | 29 |
| 30 | 31 |   |   |   |   |   |

## JUNE
| S | M | T | W | T | F | S |
|---|---|---|---|---|---|---|
|   |   | 1 | 2 | 3 | 4 | 5 |
| 6 | 7 | 8 | 9 | 10 | 11 | 12 |
| 13 | 14 | 15 | 16 | 17 | 18 | 19 |
| 20 | 21 | 22 | 23 | 24 | 25 | 26 |
| 27 | 28 | 29 | 30 |   |   |   |

## JULY
| S | M | T | W | T | F | S |
|---|---|---|---|---|---|---|
|   |   |   |   | 1 | 2 | 3 |
| 4 | 5 | 6 | 7 | 8 | 9 | 10 |
| 11 | 12 | 13 | 14 | 15 | 16 | 17 |
| 18 | 19 | 20 | 21 | 22 | 23 | 24 |
| 25 | 26 | 27 | 28 | 29 | 30 | 31 |

## AUGUST
| S | M | T | W | T | F | S |
|---|---|---|---|---|---|---|
| 1 | 2 | 3 | 4 | 5 | 6 | 7 |
| 8 | 9 | 10 | 11 | 12 | 13 | 14 |
| 15 | 16 | 17 | 18 | 19 | 20 | 21 |
| 22 | 23 | 24 | 25 | 26 | 27 | 28 |
| 29 | 30 | 31 |   |   |   |   |

## SEPTEMBER
| S | M | T | W | T | F | S |
|---|---|---|---|---|---|---|
|   |   |   | 1 | 2 | 3 | 4 |
| 5 | 6 | 7 | 8 | 9 | 10 | 11 |
| 12 | 13 | 14 | 15 | 16 | 17 | 18 |
| 19 | 20 | 21 | 22 | 23 | 24 | 25 |
| 26 | 27 | 28 | 29 | 30 |   |   |

## OCTOBER
| S | M | T | W | T | F | S |
|---|---|---|---|---|---|---|
|   |   |   |   |   | 1 | 2 |
| 3 | 4 | 5 | 6 | 7 | 8 | 9 |
| 10 | 11 | 12 | 13 | 14 | 15 | 16 |
| 17 | 18 | 19 | 20 | 21 | 22 | 23 |
| 24 | 25 | 26 | 27 | 28 | 29 | 30 |
| 31 |   |   |   |   |   |   |

## NOVEMBER
| S | M | T | W | T | F | S |
|---|---|---|---|---|---|---|
|   | 1 | 2 | 3 | 4 | 5 | 6 |
| 7 | 8 | 9 | 10 | 11 | 12 | 13 |
| 14 | 15 | 16 | 17 | 18 | 19 | 20 |
| 21 | 22 | 23 | 24 | 25 | 26 | 27 |
| 28 | 29 | 30 |   |   |   |   |

## DECEMBER
| S | M | T | W | T | F | S |
|---|---|---|---|---|---|---|
|   |   |   | 1 | 2 | 3 | 4 |
| 5 | 6 | 7 | 8 | 9 | 10 | 11 |
| 12 | 13 | 14 | 15 | 16 | 17 | 18 |
| 19 | 20 | 21 | 22 | 23 | 24 | 25 |
| 26 | 27 | 28 | 29 | 30 | 31 |   |

# 2003

## JANUARY
| S | M | T | W | T | F | S |
|---|---|---|---|---|---|---|
|   |   |   | 1 | 2 | 3 | 4 |
| 5 | 6 | 7 | 8 | 9 | 10 | 11 |
| 12 | 13 | 14 | 15 | 16 | 17 | 18 |
| 19 | 20 | 21 | 22 | 23 | 24 | 25 |
| 26 | 27 | 28 | 29 | 30 | 31 |   |

## FEBRUARY
| S | M | T | W | T | F | S |
|---|---|---|---|---|---|---|
|   |   |   |   |   |   | 1 |
| 2 | 3 | 4 | 5 | 6 | 7 | 8 |
| 9 | 10 | 11 | 12 | 13 | 14 | 15 |
| 16 | 17 | 18 | 19 | 20 | 21 | 22 |
| 23 | 24 | 25 | 26 | 27 | 28 |   |

## MARCH
| S | M | T | W | T | F | S |
|---|---|---|---|---|---|---|
|   |   |   |   |   |   | 1 |
| 2 | 3 | 4 | 5 | 6 | 7 | 8 |
| 9 | 10 | 11 | 12 | 13 | 14 | 15 |
| 16 | 17 | 18 | 19 | 20 | 21 | 22 |
| 23 | 24 | 25 | 26 | 27 | 28 | 29 |
| 30 | 31 |   |   |   |   |   |

## APRIL
| S | M | T | W | T | F | S |
|---|---|---|---|---|---|---|
|   |   | 1 | 2 | 3 | 4 | 5 |
| 6 | 7 | 8 | 9 | 10 | 11 | 12 |
| 13 | 14 | 15 | 16 | 17 | 18 | 19 |
| 20 | 21 | 22 | 23 | 24 | 25 | 26 |
| 27 | 28 | 29 | 30 |   |   |   |

## MAY
| S | M | T | W | T | F | S |
|---|---|---|---|---|---|---|
|   |   |   |   | 1 | 2 | 3 |
| 4 | 5 | 6 | 7 | 8 | 9 | 10 |
| 11 | 12 | 13 | 14 | 15 | 16 | 17 |
| 18 | 19 | 20 | 21 | 22 | 23 | 24 |
| 25 | 26 | 27 | 28 | 29 | 30 | 31 |

## JUNE
| S | M | T | W | T | F | S |
|---|---|---|---|---|---|---|
| 1 | 2 | 3 | 4 | 5 | 6 | 7 |
| 8 | 9 | 10 | 11 | 12 | 13 | 14 |
| 15 | 16 | 17 | 18 | 19 | 20 | 21 |
| 22 | 23 | 24 | 25 | 26 | 27 | 28 |
| 29 | 30 |   |   |   |   |   |

## JULY
| S | M | T | W | T | F | S |
|---|---|---|---|---|---|---|
|   |   | 1 | 2 | 3 | 4 | 5 |
| 6 | 7 | 8 | 9 | 10 | 11 | 12 |
| 13 | 14 | 15 | 16 | 17 | 18 | 19 |
| 20 | 21 | 22 | 23 | 24 | 25 | 26 |
| 27 | 28 | 29 | 30 | 31 |   |   |

## AUGUST
| S | M | T | W | T | F | S |
|---|---|---|---|---|---|---|
|   |   |   |   |   | 1 | 2 |
| 3 | 4 | 5 | 6 | 7 | 8 | 9 |
| 10 | 11 | 12 | 13 | 14 | 15 | 16 |
| 17 | 18 | 19 | 20 | 21 | 22 | 23 |
| 24 | 25 | 26 | 27 | 28 | 29 | 30 |
| 31 |   |   |   |   |   |   |

## SEPTEMBER
| S | M | T | W | T | F | S |
|---|---|---|---|---|---|---|
|   | 1 | 2 | 3 | 4 | 5 | 6 |
| 7 | 8 | 9 | 10 | 11 | 12 | 13 |
| 14 | 15 | 16 | 17 | 18 | 19 | 20 |
| 21 | 22 | 23 | 24 | 25 | 26 | 27 |
| 28 | 29 | 30 |   |   |   |   |

## OCTOBER
| S | M | T | W | T | F | S |
|---|---|---|---|---|---|---|
|   |   |   | 1 | 2 | 3 | 4 |
| 5 | 6 | 7 | 8 | 9 | 10 | 11 |
| 12 | 13 | 14 | 15 | 16 | 17 | 18 |
| 19 | 20 | 21 | 22 | 23 | 24 | 25 |
| 26 | 27 | 28 | 29 | 30 | 31 |   |

## NOVEMBER
| S | M | T | W | T | F | S |
|---|---|---|---|---|---|---|
|   |   |   |   |   |   | 1 |
| 2 | 3 | 4 | 5 | 6 | 7 | 8 |
| 9 | 10 | 11 | 12 | 13 | 14 | 15 |
| 16 | 17 | 18 | 19 | 20 | 21 | 22 |
| 23 | 24 | 25 | 26 | 27 | 28 | 29 |
| 30 |   |   |   |   |   |   |

## DECEMBER
| S | M | T | W | T | F | S |
|---|---|---|---|---|---|---|
|   | 1 | 2 | 3 | 4 | 5 | 6 |
| 7 | 8 | 9 | 10 | 11 | 12 | 13 |
| 14 | 15 | 16 | 17 | 18 | 19 | 20 |
| 21 | 22 | 23 | 24 | 25 | 26 | 27 |
| 28 | 29 | 30 | 31 |   |   |   |

# 2005

## JANUARY
| S | M | T | W | T | F | S |
|---|---|---|---|---|---|---|
|   |   |   |   |   |   | 1 |
| 2 | 3 | 4 | 5 | 6 | 7 | 8 |
| 9 | 10 | 11 | 12 | 13 | 14 | 15 |
| 16 | 17 | 18 | 19 | 20 | 21 | 22 |
| 23 | 24 | 25 | 26 | 27 | 28 | 29 |
| 30 | 31 |   |   |   |   |   |

## FEBRUARY
| S | M | T | W | T | F | S |
|---|---|---|---|---|---|---|
|   |   | 1 | 2 | 3 | 4 | 5 |
| 6 | 7 | 8 | 9 | 10 | 11 | 12 |
| 13 | 14 | 15 | 16 | 17 | 18 | 19 |
| 20 | 21 | 22 | 23 | 24 | 25 | 26 |
| 27 | 28 |   |   |   |   |   |

## MARCH
| S | M | T | W | T | F | S |
|---|---|---|---|---|---|---|
|   |   | 1 | 2 | 3 | 4 | 5 |
| 6 | 7 | 8 | 9 | 10 | 11 | 12 |
| 13 | 14 | 15 | 16 | 17 | 18 | 19 |
| 20 | 21 | 22 | 23 | 24 | 25 | 26 |
| 27 | 28 | 29 | 30 | 31 |   |   |

## APRIL
| S | M | T | W | T | F | S |
|---|---|---|---|---|---|---|
|   |   |   |   |   | 1 | 2 |
| 3 | 4 | 5 | 6 | 7 | 8 | 9 |
| 10 | 11 | 12 | 13 | 14 | 15 | 16 |
| 17 | 18 | 19 | 20 | 21 | 22 | 23 |
| 24 | 25 | 26 | 27 | 28 | 29 | 30 |

## MAY
| S | M | T | W | T | F | S |
|---|---|---|---|---|---|---|
| 1 | 2 | 3 | 4 | 5 | 6 | 7 |
| 8 | 9 | 10 | 11 | 12 | 13 | 14 |
| 15 | 16 | 17 | 18 | 19 | 20 | 21 |
| 22 | 23 | 24 | 25 | 26 | 27 | 28 |
| 29 | 30 | 31 |   |   |   |   |

## JUNE
| S | M | T | W | T | F | S |
|---|---|---|---|---|---|---|
|   |   |   | 1 | 2 | 3 | 4 |
| 5 | 6 | 7 | 8 | 9 | 10 | 11 |
| 12 | 13 | 14 | 15 | 16 | 17 | 18 |
| 19 | 20 | 21 | 22 | 23 | 24 | 25 |
| 26 | 27 | 28 | 29 | 30 |   |   |

## JULY
| S | M | T | W | T | F | S |
|---|---|---|---|---|---|---|
|   |   |   |   |   | 1 | 2 |
| 3 | 4 | 5 | 6 | 7 | 8 | 9 |
| 10 | 11 | 12 | 13 | 14 | 15 | 16 |
| 17 | 18 | 19 | 20 | 21 | 22 | 23 |
| 24 | 25 | 26 | 27 | 28 | 29 | 30 |
| 31 |   |   |   |   |   |   |

## AUGUST
| S | M | T | W | T | F | S |
|---|---|---|---|---|---|---|
|   | 1 | 2 | 3 | 4 | 5 | 6 |
| 7 | 8 | 9 | 10 | 11 | 12 | 13 |
| 14 | 15 | 16 | 17 | 18 | 19 | 20 |
| 21 | 22 | 23 | 24 | 25 | 26 | 27 |
| 28 | 29 | 30 | 31 |   |   |   |

## SEPTEMBER
| S | M | T | W | T | F | S |
|---|---|---|---|---|---|---|
|   |   |   |   | 1 | 2 | 3 |
| 4 | 5 | 6 | 7 | 8 | 9 | 10 |
| 11 | 12 | 13 | 14 | 15 | 16 | 17 |
| 18 | 19 | 20 | 21 | 22 | 23 | 24 |
| 25 | 26 | 27 | 28 | 29 | 30 |   |

## OCTOBER
| S | M | T | W | T | F | S |
|---|---|---|---|---|---|---|
|   |   |   |   |   |   | 1 |
| 2 | 3 | 4 | 5 | 6 | 7 | 8 |
| 9 | 10 | 11 | 12 | 13 | 14 | 15 |
| 16 | 17 | 18 | 19 | 20 | 21 | 22 |
| 23 | 24 | 25 | 26 | 27 | 28 | 29 |
| 30 | 31 |   |   |   |   |   |

## NOVEMBER
| S | M | T | W | T | F | S |
|---|---|---|---|---|---|---|
|   |   | 1 | 2 | 3 | 4 | 5 |
| 6 | 7 | 8 | 9 | 10 | 11 | 12 |
| 13 | 14 | 15 | 16 | 17 | 18 | 19 |
| 20 | 21 | 22 | 23 | 24 | 25 | 26 |
| 27 | 28 | 29 | 30 |   |   |   |

## DECEMBER
| S | M | T | W | T | F | S |
|---|---|---|---|---|---|---|
|   |   |   |   | 1 | 2 | 3 |
| 4 | 5 | 6 | 7 | 8 | 9 | 10 |
| 11 | 12 | 13 | 14 | 15 | 16 | 17 |
| 18 | 19 | 20 | 21 | 22 | 23 | 24 |
| 25 | 26 | 27 | 28 | 29 | 30 | 31 |

# Telephone Numbers

# Birthdays

# Personal Profile

Name —————————————————————————

Address ———————————————————————

——————————————————— Phone ——————

Business Address ——————————————————

——————————————————— Phone ——————

## Personal Data

Driver's Lic. #————————— Attorney——————

Lic. Plate #————————— Physician ——————

Vehicle Reg. #————————— Medical Alert————

Social Security # ————————— Blood Type————

Passport # ————————— Other——————

## Insurance

Auto Policy #————————— Company—————

Agent ————————— Phone —————

Health Policy #————————— Company—————

Agent ————————— Phone —————

Homeowner's Policy #————————— Company—————

Agent ————————— Phone —————

## In Case of Emergency Notify

Name—————————————————————

Address—————————————————————

Relationship————————— Phone —————

# Family Information

| Measurements for: | Dad | Mom | | | | | |
|---|---|---|---|---|---|---|---|
| Belt | | | | | | | |
| Blouse | | | | | | | |
| Coat | | | | | | | |
| Dress | | | | | | | |
| Pants | | | | | | | |
| Shirt | | | | | | | |
| Neck | | | | | | | |
| Sleeve | | | | | | | |
| Shoe | | | | | | | |
| Suit | | | | | | | |
| Sweater | | | | | | | |
| Swimsuit | | | | | | | |
| Underwear | | | | | | | |
| Favorite Colors | | | | | | | |

#  Addresses

Name _____

Address _____

_____ Phone _____

Name _____

Address _____

_____ Phone _____

Name _____

Address _____

_____ Phone _____

Name _____

Address _____

_____ Phone _____

Name _____

Address _____

_____ Phone _____

Name _____

Address _____

_____ Phone _____

# Addresses

Name _____

Address _____

_____ Phone _____

Name _____

Address _____

_____ Phone _____

Name _____

Address _____

_____ Phone _____

Name _____

Address _____

_____ Phone _____

Name _____

Address _____

_____ Phone _____

Name _____

Address _____

_____ Phone _____

# Addresses

Name _____

Address _____

_____ Phone _____

Name _____

Address _____

_____ Phone _____

Name _____

Address _____

_____ Phone _____

Name _____

Address _____

_____ Phone _____

Name _____

Address _____

_____ Phone _____

Name _____

Address _____

_____ Phone _____

# Addresses

Name _____

Address _____

_____ Phone _____

Name _____

Address _____

_____ Phone _____

Name _____

Address _____

_____ Phone _____

Name _____

Address _____

_____ Phone _____

Name _____

Address _____

_____ Phone _____

Name _____

Address _____

_____ Phone _____

# Addresses

Name _____

Address _____

_____ Phone _____

Name _____

Address _____

_____ Phone _____

Name _____

Address _____

_____ Phone _____

Name _____

Address _____

_____ Phone _____

Name _____

Address _____

_____ Phone _____

Name _____

Address _____

_____ Phone _____

# 2004 Dates to Remember

## January
1 New Year's Day
19 Martin Luther King Jr.'s
   Birthday Observed

## February
12 Lincoln's Birthday
14 Valentine's Day
16 Presidents' Day
22 Washington's Birthday
25 Ash Wednesday

## March
17 St. Patrick's Day
20 Spring Begins

## April
4 Palm Sunday
6 Passover
9 Good Friday
11 Easter

## May
6 National Day of Prayer
9 Mother's Day
15 Armed Forces Day
31 Memorial Day Observed

## June
14 Flag Day
20 Father's Day
20 Summer Begins

## July
4 Independence Day

## August
2 Friendship Day

## September
6 Labor Day
12 Grandparent's Day
16 Rosh Hashanah
22 Autumn Begins
25 Yom Kippur

## October
11 Columbus Day Observed
16 Boss Day
16 Sweetest Day
24 Mother-in-Law Day

## November
2 Election Day
11 Veterans Day
25 Thanksgiving
28 First Sunday of Advent

## December
8 First Day of Hanukkah
21 Winter Begins
24 Christmas Eve
25 Christmas Day

# Wedding Anniversary Gifts

|  | TRADITIONAL | MODERN |
|---|---|---|
| First | Paper | Clocks |
| Second | Cotton | China |
| Third | Leather | Crystal/Glass |
| Fourth | Fruit/Flowers | Appliances |
| Fifth | Wood | Silverware |
| Sixth | Candy/Iron | Wood |
| Seventh | Wool/Copper | Desk Sets |
| Eighth | Bronze/Pottery | Linens/Lace |
| Ninth | Pottery/Willow | Leather |
| Tenth | Tin/Aluminum | Diamond Jewelry |
| Eleventh | Steel | Fashion Jewelry |
| Twelfth | Silk/Linen | Pearls |
| Thirteenth | Lace | Textiles/Furs |
| Fourteenth | Ivory | Gold Jewelry |
| Fifteenth | Crystal | Watches |
| Sixteenth |  | Silver Hollowware |
| Seventeenth |  | Furniture |
| Eighteenth |  | Porcelain |
| Nineteenth |  | Bronze |
| Twentieth | China | Platinum |
| Twenty-fifth | Silver | Silver |
| Thirtieth | Pearl | Diamond |
| Thirty-fifth | Coral | Jade |
| Fortieth | Ruby | Ruby |
| Forty-fifth | Sapphire | Sapphire |
| Fiftieth | Gold | Gold |
| Fifty-fifth | Emerald | Emerald |
| Sixtieth | Diamond | Diamond |
| Seventy-fifth | Diamond | Diamond |

For more information contact the Web site of
**Joni and Friends** at www.joniandfriends.org

or you can write or call us at
**Joni and Friends**, P.O. Box 3333,
Agoura Hills, CA 91376, USA
818-707-5664